CLEAN AND CRAFTY

DISHCLOTHS FOR ALL SEASONS

Photography by Amy Setter

Printed in the United States of America

First Printing, 2018

ISBN 978-1-62767-183-5

Versa Press, Inc
800-447-7829

www.versapress.com

CONTENTS

SPRING

In the Spring, I have counted 136 different kinds of weather inside of 24 hours.

- Mark Twain

LEAF DISHCLOTH

by Allyson Dykhuizen

Celebrate spring with this sweet dishcloth! This dishcloth is worked from the bottom up, starting with the stem loop and working in a Garter stitch pattern to the top. Slipping the first stitch of every row keeps a tidy edge. Knit it up in a green yarn to greet new leaves on your tree or try it in an orange or yellow to celebrate the fall colors.

FINISHED MEASUREMENTS
6.5" tall plus 2" loop x 8" wide

YARN
Knit Picks CotLin (70% Tanguis Cotton, 30% Linen; 123 yards/50g):
Sprout 24462, 1 ball

NEEDLES
US 5 (3.75mm) DPNs and straight or circular needles, or size to obtain gauge

NOTIONS
Yarn Needle

GAUGE
22 sts and 36 rows = 4" in Garter st, blocked

Notes:
You can change to straight needles once you get too many stitches on your DPNs.
I-Cord (worked over 3 sts on DPNs)
CO 3 sts.
Row 1: K3 onto right needle as usual. Without turning work and WYIB, slide sts to right end of DPN. This is now your left needle.
Rep Row 1 for pattern.

DIRECTIONS

Stem
With DPNs CO 3 sts. Work in I-cord for 4.5".
Next Row (RS): K3, PU & K3 sts from the CO sts at the opposite end of the I-Cord, creating a loop. 6 sts.
Knit 1 WS row.

Leaf
Row 1 (RS): CO 12 at beginning of row, K to end. 18 sts.
Row 2 (WS): CO 12 at beginning of row, K to end. 30 sts.
Rows 3 - 8: K.
Row 9 (RS): Sl1, KFB, K to last 2 sts, KFB, K1. 2 sts inc. 32 sts.
Row 10 (WS): K.
Rep last 2 rows 3 more times. 38 sts.
Row 17: Sl 1, KFB, K to last 2 sts, KFB, K1. 2 sts inc. 40 sts.
Rows 18-20: K.
Rep last 4 rows 2 more times. 44 sts.
Rows 29 - 36: K.
Row 37 (RS): BO 10, K to end. 34 sts.
Row 38 (WS): BO 10, K to end. 24 sts.
Row 39: Sl 1, K2tog, K to 3 sts from end, K2tog, K1. 2 sts dec. 22 sts.
Rows 40-42: K.
Rep last 4 rows 2 more times. 18 sts.
Row 51 (RS): Sl 1, K2tog, K to 3 sts from end, K2tog, K1. 2 sts dec. 16 sts.
Row 52 (WS): K.
Rep last 2 rows 2 more times. 12 sts.
Row 57: Sl 1, K2tog, K to 3 sts from end, K2tog, K1. 2 sts dec. 10 sts.
Rep last row twice more. 6 sts.
BO remaining sts.

Finishing
Weave in ends, wash and block to measurements.

SUNFLOWER DISHCLOTH

by Allyson Dykhuizen

Bring a smile to anyone's face with this cheerful dishcloth. Worked from the center out, the Sunflower Dishcloth is quick and easy and a fun project for adventurous beginners.

FINISHED MEASUREMENTS
9.75" across including petals.

YARN
Knit Picks CotLin (70% Tanguis Cotton, 30% Linen; 123 yards/50g): C1 Coffee 24138, C2 Canary 24837, 1 ball each

NEEDLES
US 5 (3.75mm) DPNs, or size to obtain gauge

NOTIONS
Marker
Yarn Needle
Scrap Yarn (optional)

GAUGE
22 sts and 36 rnds = 4" in Garter st, blocked

Notes:
This dishcloth is worked from the center out. Stitches are held as petals are worked around the center of the flower, or head.

DIRECTIONS

Sunflower Head
With C1, CO 6 sts. Divide sts evenly between 3 DPNs, 2 sts each needle, PM and join to work in the round.
Rnds 1 - 21 odd rnds only: P.
Rnd 2: KFB around. 12 sts.
Rnd 4: (K1, KFB) around. 18 sts.
Rnd 6: (K2, KFB) around. 24 sts.
Rnd 8: (K3, KFB) around. 30 sts.
Rnd 10: (K4, KFB) around. 36 sts.
Rnd 12: (K5, KFB) around. 42 sts.
Rnd 14: (K6, KFB) around. 48 sts.
Rnd 16: (K7, KFB) around. 54 sts.
Rnd 18: (K8, KFB) around. 60 sts.
Rnd 20: (K9, KFB) around. 66 sts.
Rnd 22: (K10, KFB) around. 72 sts.
Rnd 23: (P2tog, P34) around. 70 sts.
Rnd 24: K.
While working petals you can move unworked sts to scrap yarn, or leave them unworked on your needles. Cut C1 and work with only C2 for Petals.

Petals
Row 1 (RS): With RS facing, K7, turn to work next WS row.
Row 2 (WS): K1, P1, K3, P1, K1.
Rep these 2 rows two more times.
Row 7 (RS): K3, KFB, K3. 8 sts.
Row 8 (WS): K1, P1, K4, P1, K1.
Row 9: K.
Row 10: K1, P1, K4, P1, K1.
Rep rows 9-10 two more times.
Row 15: K3, K2tog, K3. 7 sts.
Row 16: K1, P1, K3, P1, K1.
Row 17: K2, Sk2p, K2. 5 sts.
Row 18: (K1, P1) twice, K1.
Row 19: K1, Sk2p, K1. 3 sts.
Row 20: K1, P1, K1.
Cut yarn and pull through remaining sts to secure.
Returning to unworked sts and beginning with the next 7 RS sts, work next Petal. Continue working around Sunflower Head in this manner until all sts have been worked. 10 Petals total.

Finishing
Weave in ends, wash and block to measurements.

TULIP DISHCLOTH

by Allyson Dykhuizen

In spring, beautiful tulips are found everywhere - a bright burst of color after a long cold winter. Celebrate your love of flowers with this fun dishcloth! Starting with an I-cord loop, it blooms with a striking garter stitch pattern. Each petal is knit separately, with the remaining stitches held on the needles so there's no seaming. Knit a few and deck out your kitchen in colorful springtime fun.

FINISHED MEASUREMENTS

6.5" tall body plus 2" loop x 6.25" wide

YARN

Knit Picks CotLin (70% Tanguis Cotton, 30% Linen; 123 yards/50g): C1 Cerise 24835, C2 Sprout 24462, 1 ball each

NEEDLES

US 5 (3.75mm) DPNs and straight or circular needles, or size to obtain gauge

NOTIONS

Yarn Needle

GAUGE

22 sts and 36 rows = 4" in Garter st, blocked

Notes:

This dishcloth is worked from the bottom up, starting with the stem loop and working in a Garter stitch pattern to the top. Change to straight or circular needles once you get too many stitches on your DPNs.

Right Twist Purl (RTP)

Skip the next st, K into the front of the second st on the left needle leaving the first st on the left hand needle. P skipped st, Sl both sts off the needle - 2 sts worked.

Left Twist Purl (LTP)

Skip the next st, reach behind the first st and P into the back of the second st on the left needle, leaving the first st on the left hand needle. K skipped st, slip both sts off the needle - 2 sts worked.

I-Cord (worked over 3 sts on DPNs)

Row 1: K3 onto right needle as usual. Without turning work and WYIB, slide sts to right end of DPN. This is now your left needle.
Rep Row 1 for pattern.

DIRECTIONS

Stem

With C2 and DPNs, CO 3 sts. Work in I-Cord for 4.5".
Next Row (RS): K3, PU & K3 sts from the CO sts at the opposite end of the I-Cord, creating a loop. 6 sts.
Cut C2.
Change to C1.
Next Row (WS): P.

Flower

Row 1 (RS): K1, KFB, K1, KFB, KFB, K1. 9 sts.
Row 2 (WS): K1, P1, KFB, K1, P1, K1, KFB, P1, K1. 11 sts.
Rows 3, 5, 7, 9 and 11: K2, KFB, K to last 3 sts, KFB, K2. 2 sts inc.
Row 4: K1, P1, KFB, K3, P1, K3, KFB, P1, K1. 15 sts.
Row 6: K1, P1, KFB, K5, P1, K5, KFB, P1, K1. 19 sts.
Row 8: K1, P1, KFB, K7, P1, K7, KFB, P1, K1. 23 sts.
Row 10: K1, P1, KFB, K9, P1, K9, KFB, P1, K1. 27 sts.
Row 12: K1, P1, KFB, K11, P1, K11, KFB, P1, K1. 31 sts.
Row 13: K14, RTP, with the left hand needle PU the second leg of the st below the st just worked and K into the back loop, K11, K2tog, K2. 31 sts.
Row 14: K1, P1, KFB, K11, P1, K1, P1, K11, KFB, P1, K1. 33 sts.
Row 15: K14, RTP, P1, LTP, K14.
Row 16: K1, P1, KFB, K11, P1, K3, P1, K11, KFB, P1, K1. 35 sts.
Row 17: K.
Row 18: K1, P1, K13, P1, K3, P1, K13, P1, K1.
Rep Rows 17-18 twice more.
Row 23 (RS): K14, RTP, K3, LTP, K14.
Row 24 (WS): K1, P1, K12, P1, K5, P1, K12, P1, K1.
Row 25: K.
Rep Rows 24-25 twice, then Row 24 once more.
Row 31 (RS): K13, RTP, K5, LTP, K13.
Row 32 (WS): K1, P1, K11, P1, K7, P1, K11, P1, K1.
Row 33: K12, RTP, K7, LTP, K12.
Row 34: K1, P1, K10, P1, K9, P1, K10, P1, K1.
Row 35: K11, RTP, K9, LTP, K11.
Row 36: K1, P1, K9, P1, K11, P1, K9, P1, K1.
Row 37: K10, RTP, K11, LTP, K10.
Row 38: K1, P1, K8, P1, K13, P1, K8, P1, K1.
Row 39: K9, RTP, K13, LTP, K9.
Row 40: K1, P1, K7, P1, K15, P1, K7, P1, K1.
Row 41: K.
Row 42: Same as Row 40.
Row 43: K8, RTP, K15, LTP, K8.
Row 44: K1, P1, K6, P1, K17, P1, K6, P1, K1.
Row 45: K.
Row 46: Same as Row 44.

Right Petal

Row 47 (RS): K6, K2tog, K2; turn, leaving unworked sts on needle. 9 sts.
Row 48 (WS): K1, P1, K5, P1, K1.
Row 49: K.
Rep Rows 48-49 once, then rep Row 48 once more.
Row 53: K5, K2tog, K2. 8 sts.
Row 54: K1, P1, K4, P1, K1.
Row 55: K4, K2tog, K2. 7 sts.
Row 56: K1, P1, K2tog, K1, P1, K1. 6 sts.
Row 57: K2, K2tog, K2. 5 sts.
Row 58: K1, P1, P2tog TBL, K1. 4 sts.
Row 59: K1, K2tog, K1. 3 sts.
Cut yarn and pull tail through Right Petal sts to secure.

Center Petal

With RS facing, rejoin C1.

Row 47 (RS): K2, SSK, K7, K2tog, K2; turn, leaving unworked sts on needle. 13 sts.

Row 48 (WS): K1, P1, K9, P1, K1.

Row 49: K.

Rep Rows 48-49 once, then rep Row 48 once more.

Row 53: K2, SSK, K5, K2tog, K2. 11 sts.

Row 54: K1, P1, K7, P1, K1.

Row 55: K2, SSK, K3, K2tog, K2. 9 sts.

Row 56: K1, P1, K2tog, K1, K2tog, P1, K1. 7 sts.

Row 57: K2, Sl 1, K2tog, PSSO, K2. 5 sts.

Row 58: K1, P1, K1, P1, K1.

Row 59: K1, Sl 1, K2tog, PSSO, K1. 3 sts.

Cut yarn and pull tail through Center Petal sts to secure.

Left Petal

With RS facing, rejoin C1 and work remaining sts.

Row 47 (RS): K2, SSK, K to end. 9 sts.

Row 48 (WS): K1, P1, K to last 2 sts, P1, K1.

Row 49: K.

Rep Rows 48-49 once, then rep Row 48 once more.

Rep Rows 47-48 once. 8 sts.

Rep Row 47. 7 sts.

Row 56: K1, P1, K1, K2tog, P1, K1. 6 sts.

Row 57: K2, K2tog, K2. 5 sts.

Row 58: K1, P2tog, P1, K1. 4 sts.

Row 59: K1, K2tog, K1. 3 sts.

Cut yarn and pull tail through remaining sts to secure.

Finishing

Weave in ends, wash and block to measurements.

KINGLY WASHCLOTH

by Emily Ringelman

You'll feel like royalty every time you use this cute project! This washcloth is shaped like a crown, with five points at the top and a band with bobbles at the bottom. Non-rolling double seed stitch makes up the body of the crown.

FINISHED MEASUREMENTS

7.5" Square

YARN

Knit Picks Dishie (100% Cotton; 190 yards/100g): Crème Brûlèe 25404, 1 ball

NEEDLES

US 7 (4.5mm) straight or circular needles, or size to obtain gauge

NOTIONS

Yarn Needle

Waste Yarn or Stitch Holder (optional)

GAUGE

20 sts and 28 rows = 4" over St st worked flat, blocked

Notes:

This dishcloth is shaped like a crown, with five points at the top and a band with bobbles at the bottom. Non-rolling double seed stitch makes up the body of the crown.

Double Seed Stitch (worked flat over even number of sts)

Rows 1 & 2: (K1, P1) to end.

Rows 3 & 4: (P1, K1) to end.

Make Bobble (MB)

K into the front, back, front, back, and front of the same st (5 sts); turn and P5; turn and K5; pass 4 sts over the left-most st.

DIRECTIONS

CO 37 sts. K 4 rows.

Row 1 (WS): K2, P to last 2 sts, K2.

Row 2 (RS): K4, (MB, K6) four times, MB, K4.

Row 3: Rep Row 1.

Rows 4 - 7: K.

Row 8: Work Double Seed Stitch Row 1 to last st, K1.

Row 9: P1, work Double Seed Stitch Row 2 to end.

Row 10: Work Double Seed Stitch Row 3 to last st, P1.

Row 11: K1, work Double Seed Stitch Row 4 to end.

Rep the last 4 rows until piece measures 6.75" from CO edge, ending after Row 4 of Double Seed Stitch.

Rightmost Point

Next Row (RS): K1, P1, K1, K2tog. Place unworked sts on the left needle on waste yarn, st holder or leave on left needle, but ignore for now. 4 sts.

Next Row (WS): P2tog, K1, P1. 3 sts.

Next Row: K1, K2tog. 2 sts.

Next Row: P2tog. 1 st.

Break yarn and draw through st.

Right Middle Point

Place next 7 sts on left working needle. Join yarn to work a RS row.

Row 1 (RS): SSK, P1, K1, P1, K2tog. 5 sts.

Row 2 (WS): P2tog, P1, P2tog TBL. 3 sts.

Row 3: Sl1, K2tog, PSSO. 1 st.

Break yarn and draw through st.

Middle Point

Place next 13 sts on left working needle. Join yarn to work a RS row.

Row 1 (RS): SSK, (K1, P1) four times, K1, K2tog. 11 sts.

Row 2 (WS): P2tog, (K1, P1) three times, K1, P2tog TBL. 9 sts.

Row 3: SSK, (P1, K1) twice, P1, K2tog. 7 sts.

Row 4: P2tog, P1, K1, P1, P2tog TBL. 5 sts.

Row 5: SSK, K1, K2tog. 3 sts.

Row 6: P3tog. 1 st.

Break yarn and draw through st.

Left Middle Point

Place next 7 sts on left working needle. Join yarn to work a RS row.

Row 1: SSK, P1, K1, P1, K2tog. 5 sts.

Row 2: P2tog, P1, P2tog TBL. 3 sts.

Row 3: Sl1, K2tog, PSSO. 1 st.

Break yarn and draw through st.

Leftmost Point

Place remaining 5 sts on left needle. Join yarn to work a RS row.

Row 1: SSK, K1, P1, K1. 4 sts.

Row 2: P1, K1, P2tog TBL. 3 sts

Row 3: SSK, P1. 2 sts.

Row 4: P2tog TBL. 1 st.

Break yarn and draw through st.

Finishing

Weave in ends, wash and block.

PERFECTLY PREPPY WASHCLOTH

by Emily Ringelman

This happy washcloth will bring a smile to your face every time you see it! Featuring a sweet intarsia stripes and heart design and a garter border to keep it flat, this project is perfect to practice new knitting skills with a useful project at the end.

FINISHED MEASUREMENTS

10.5" wide x 9" high

YARN

Knit Picks Dishie (100% Cotton; 190 yards/100g): MC Clarity 27037, CC1 Blue 25787, CC2 Begonia 25790, 1 ball each

NEEDLES

US 7 (4.5mm) straight or circular needles, or size to obtain gauge

NOTIONS

Yarn Needle
Stitch Markers

GAUGE

20 sts and 28 rows = 4" over St st worked flat, blocked

Notes:

This washcloth has garter stitch borders to prevent rolling. The center features an intarsia design of stripes and a heart.

Read the charts RS rows (odd numbers) from right to left, and WS rows (even numbers) from left to right.

DIRECTIONS

With MC and straight or circular needles, CO 53. K 7 rows.

Next Row (RS): K4, PM, K to last 4 sts, PM, K4.

Next Row (WS): K4, SM, P to M, SM, K4.

Next Row: With MC, K4, SM, work Intarsia Chart Row 1 to M, SM, with MC K4.

Continue as established until Intarsia Chart is complete, joining CC1 and CC2 when necessary, and remembering to twist yarns at color changes to avoid holes. The first and last 4 sts of each row will be knit in MC.

When Intarsia Chart is complete, piece should measure approximately 8" tall.

With MC, K 7 rows, then BO K-wise.

Finishing

Weave in ends, wash and block to diagram.

Perfectly Preppy Chart

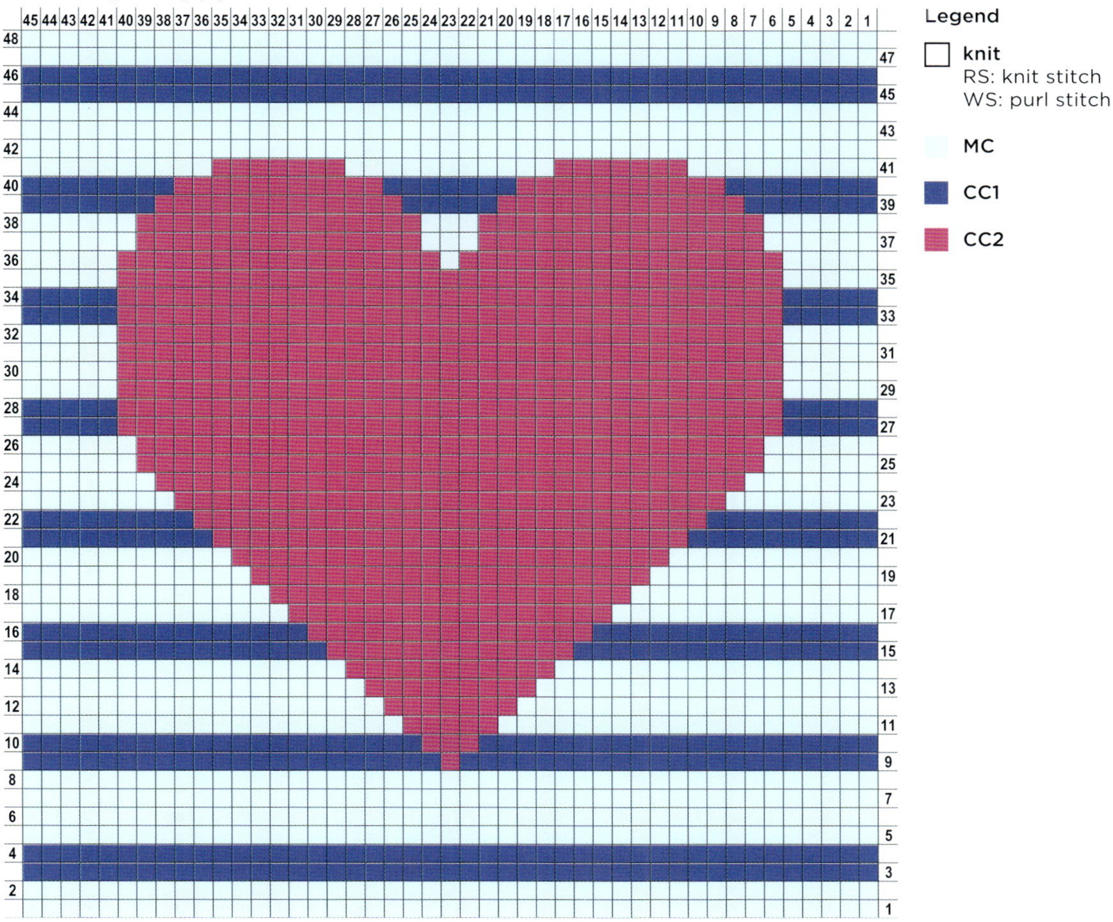

TIPSY EYELETS FACECLOTH

by Faith Schmidt

Tipsy Eyelets Facecloth is a quick and fun knit. The stitch pattern is easy to memorize, and the eyelets create a lacy texture; perfect for gift giving, or just for pampering yourself. It can easily be resized to fit your needs.

FINISHED MEASUREMENTS

Approximately 11.25" x 11", unblocked

YARN

Knit Picks CotLin (70% Cotton, 30% Linen; 123 yards/50g): Whisper 25328, 1 ball

NEEDLES

US 4 (3.5mm) straight or circular needles, or size to obtain gauge

NOTIONS

Yarn Needle

GAUGE

17 sts and 32 rows = 4" in Eyelet St, unblocked. (Exact gauge is not important to this project.)

Notes:

To resize, cast on a multiple of 22 sts plus 4, and knit to desired length.

Tipsy Eyelets Stitch (worked flat over a multiple of 22 sts plus 4)

Rows 1(RS): K.

Row 2 and all even rows: P.

Row 3: K2, *P4, (K2tog, YO, K1) twice, K2tog, YO, P10; rep from * to last 2 sts, K2.

Row 5: K2, *K3, (K2tog, YO, K1) 3 times, K10; rep from * to last 2 sts, K2.

Row 7: K2, *P2, (K2tog, YO, K1) twice, K2tog, YO, P12; rep from * to last 2 sts, K2.

Row 9: K2, *K1, (K2tog, YO, K1) 3 times, K12; rep from * to last 2 sts, K2.

Row 11: K2, *(K2tog, YO, K1) twice, K2tog, YO, P14; rep from * to last 2 sts, K2.

Row 13: K.

Row 15: K2, *P9, (K1, YO, SSK) 3 times, P4; rep from * to last 2 sts, K2.

Row 17: K2, *K11, (YO, SSK. K1) 3 times, K2; rep from * to last 2 sts, K2.

Row 19: K2, *P11, (K1, YO, SSK) 3 times, P2; rep from * to last 2 sts, K2.

Row 21: K2, *K13, (YO, SSK, K1) 3 times; rep from * to last 2 sts, K2.

Row 23: K2, *P13, (K1, YO, SSK) 3 times; rep from * to last 2 sts, K2.

Row 24: P.

DIRECTIONS

CO 48 sts, using the Long Tail CO. Knit 1 row. Work Tipsy Eyelets Pattern (Rows 1-24) 3 times total, then work Rows 1-13 once. BO K-wise on WS.

Finishing

Weave in ends, block lightly, if desired, to open up the eyelets.

Tipsy Eyelets Chart

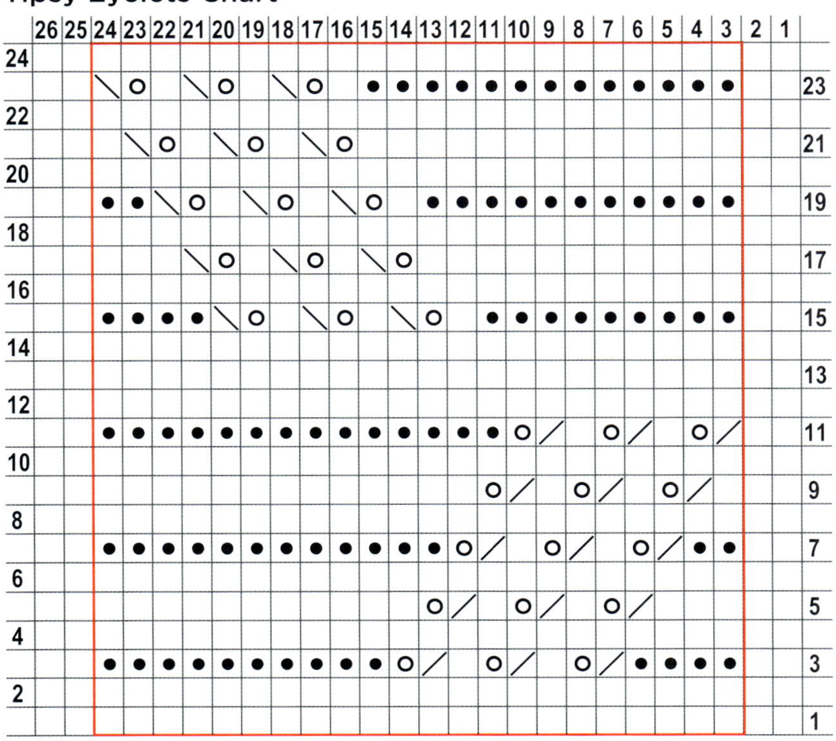

Legend:

- **knit**
  RS: knit stitch
  WS: purl stitch
- **purl**
  RS: purl stitch
  WS: knit stitch
- **k2tog**
  Knit two stitches together as one stitch
- **yo**
  Yarn Over
- **ssk**
  Slip one stitch as if to knit, slip another stitch as if to knit. Insert left-hand needle into front of these 2 stitches and knit them together

SPIRAL COLUMNS FACECLOTH

by Faith Schmidt

Spiral Columns Facecloth is created by twisting stitches; no cable needle is required. The pattern is easy to read and quick to knit. It can easily be resized to fit your needs.

FINISHED MEASUREMENTS

Approximately 9.75" square, slightly stretched.

YARN

Knit Picks CotLin (70% Tanguis Cotton, 30% Linen; 123 yards/50g): Sprout 24462, 1 ball

NEEDLES

US 4 (3.5mm) straight or circular needles, or size to obtain gauge

NOTIONS

Yarn Needle

GAUGE

21 sts and 30 rows = 4" over Spiral Columns Stitch, slightly stretched. Exact gauge is not important to this project

Notes:

Left Twist (LT)

Skip the first st on the left needle, and knit the second st TBL, without dropping the stitch off the needle. Slip the first stitch P-wise, and then drop the second st off the needle.

To resize, CO a multiple of 7 plus 2 sts, and knit to desired length.

Spiral Columns Stitch (worked flat over a multiple of 7 plus 2 sts)

Row 1 and all WS Rows: K2, *P5, K2, repeat from * to end of row.
Row 2: P2, *LT, K3, P2, repeat from * to end of row.
Row 4: P2, *K1, LT, K2, P2, repeat from * to end of row.
Row 6: P2, *K2, LT, K1, P2, repeat from * to end of row.
Row 8: P2, *K3, LT, P2, repeat from * to end of row.
Repeat Rows 1-8 for pattern.

DIRECTIONS

CO 51 sts, using the Long Tail CO.
Work Rows 1-8 of the Spiral Columns Stitch Pattern 9 times total.
BO (WS) P-wise.

Finishing

Weave in ends. Block lightly to open up the pattern.

WILDROSE DISHCLOTH

by Kalurah Hudson

This pretty dishcloth is cast on from the center using a crochet hook and knit in the round. The increases form a square shape, embellished with four lace rosebuds. A picot trim adds a delicate touch.

FINISHED MEASUREMENTS

11" square, blocked

YARN

Knit Picks Comfy Worsted (75% Pima Cotton, 25% Acrylic; 109 yards/50g): Rosehip 25769, 1 ball

NEEDLES

US 5 (3.75mm) DPNs and 16" circular needles, or size to obtain gauge
US 4 (3.5mm) DPNs, or one size smaller than size to obtain gauge

NOTIONS

Size 3mm Crochet hook (optional for cast on)
Yarn Needle

GAUGE

14 sts and 24 rounds = 4" in St st in the round, blocked

Notes:
The Circular CO Tutorial can be seen here: http://tutorials.knitpicks.com/circular-cast-on/
The tutorial shows the new stitches picked up with a knitting needle, but a crochet hook could be used instead.

Sl2, K1, P2SSO: Sl2 sts K-wise, K1, pass Sl sts over K st. (3 sts decreased to 1.)

SSSK: Sl3 sts K-wise, one at a time, place sts back onto LH needle, K3tog TBL. (3 sts decreased to 1.)

Wildrose Chart (worked 4 times around)
Rnd 1: K1, YO, K1. (3 sts)
Rnds 2-12 Even Rnds: K.
Rnd 3: (K1, YO) x 2, K1. (5 sts)
Rnd 5: K1, YO, K3, YO, K1. (7 sts)
Rnd 7: K1, YO, K5, YO, K1. (9 sts)
Rnd 9: K1, YO, K7, YO, K1. (11 sts)
Rnd 11: K1, YO, K4, (K1, YO, K1) in one st, K4, YO, K1. (15 sts)
Rnd 13: K1, YO, K3, K3tog, YO, (K1, YO, K1) in one st, YO, SSSK, K3, YO, K1. (17 sts)
Rnd 14: K11, K1 TBL, K5.
Rnd 15: K1, YO, K2, K3tog, YO, K2tog, YO, (K1, YO, K1) in one st, YO, SSK, YO, SSSK, K2, YO, K1. (19 sts)
Rnd 16: K12, K1 TBL, K1, K TBL, K4.
Rnd 17: K1, YO, K2, (K2tog, YO) x 3, K1, (YO, SSK) x 3, K2, YO, K1. (21 sts)
Rnd 18: K12, (K1 TBL, K1) x 2, K1 TBL, K4.
Rnd 19: K1, YO, K4, (YO, K2tog) x 2, YO, Sl2, K1, P2SSO, (YO, SSK) x 2, YO, K4, YO, K1. (23 sts)
Rnd 20: K13, K1 TBL, K1, K1 TBL, K7.
Rnd 21: K1, YO, K4, (SSK, YO) x 3, K1, (YO, K2tog) x 3, K4, YO, K1. (25 sts)
Rnd 22: K6, (K1 TBL, K1) x 2, K1 TBL, K14.
Rnd 23: K1, YO, K7, (YO, SSK) x 2, K1, (K2tog, YO) x 2, K7, YO, K1. (27 sts)
Rnd 24: K10, K1 TBL, K1, K1 TBL, K14.
Rnd 25: K1, YO, K9, YO, SSK, YO, Sl2, K1, P2SSO, YO, K2tog, YO, K9, YO, K1. (29 sts)
Rnd 26: K12, K1 TBL, K16.
Rnd 27: K1, YO, K11, YO, SSK, K1, K2tog, YO, K11, YO, K1. (31 sts)
Rnd 28: K14, K1 TBL, K16.
Rnd 29: K1, YO, K13, YO, Sl2, K1, P2SSO, YO, K13, YO, K1. (33 sts)
Rnd 30: K.
Rnd 31: K1, YO, K31, YO, K1. (35 sts)
Rnd 32: K.
Rnd 33: K1, YO, K33, YO, K1. (37 sts)

DIRECTIONS

Using the Circular CO technique, CO 8 sts. Evenly distribute onto 4 DPNs. Switch to circular needles when there are too many sts to fit on DPNs comfortably.
Rnds 1-33: Work Rnds 1-33 of chart, working each rnd 4 times around.
There will be 148 sts after Rnd 33 is complete.
Rnd 34: P.
Rnd 35: (K2tog, YO) 74 times.
Rnd 36: P.
Picot BO
Using smaller DPNs, (Cable CO 2 sts, BO 5 sts, place loop back onto LH needle), rep to last st, Cable CO 2 sts, BO all sts.
Break yarn.

Finishing

Pull tail from CO tight to close up hole. Weave in ends, wash and block to finished measurements.

Wildrose Chart

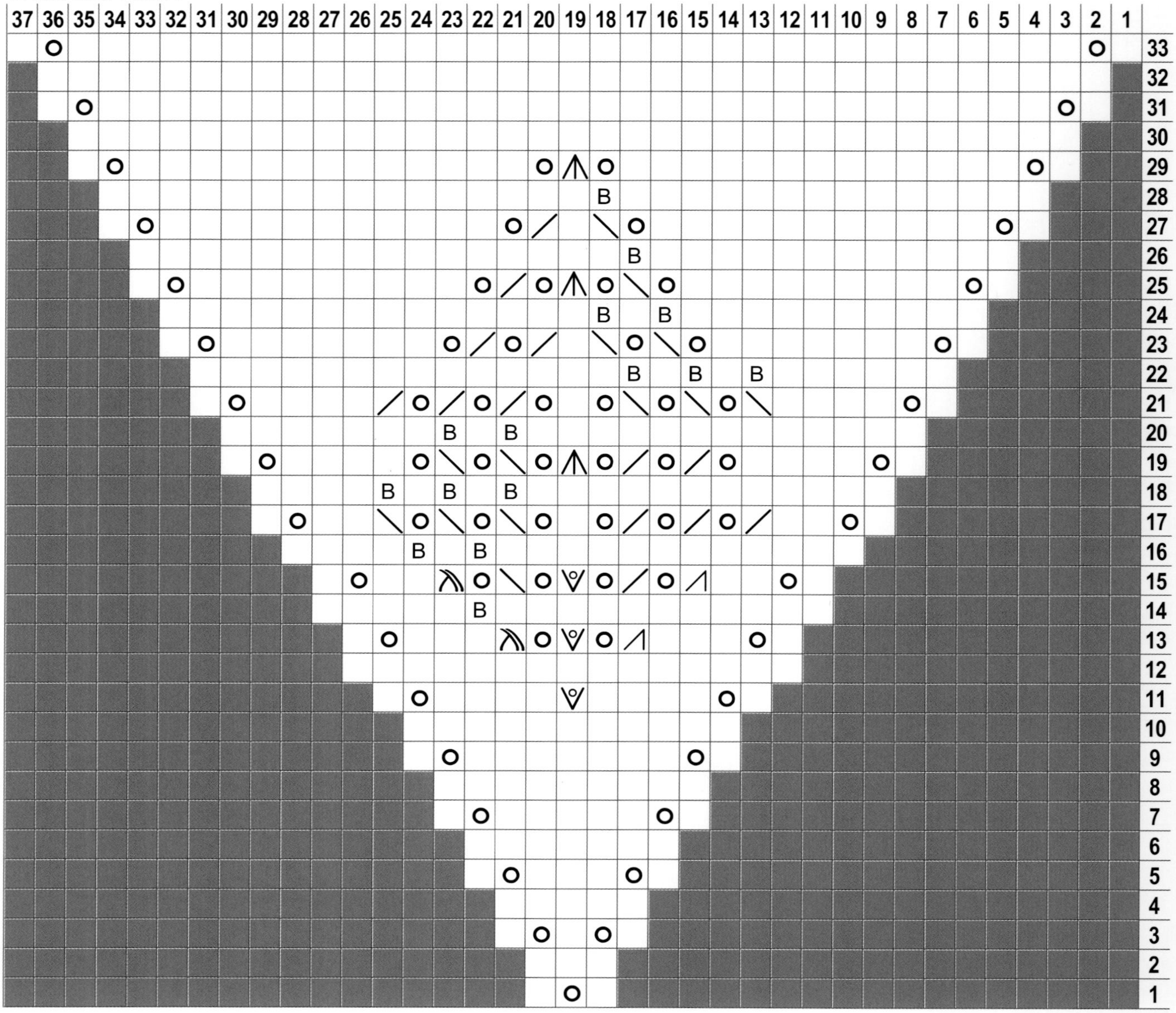

Legend

No Stitch
Placeholder - No stitch made.

knit
knit stitch

yo
Yarn Over

(k1 yo k1) in 1 st
k1 leave on needle, yo, then knit again into same st to make 3 sts from 1

k3tog
Knit three stitches together as one

sssk
(Slip 1 as if to knit) 3 times; insert left-hand needle from the front to the back of all stitches at the same time and knit them together.

knit tbl
Knit stitch through back loop

k2tog
Knit two stitches together as one stitch

ssk
Slip one stitch as if to knit, Slip another stitch as if to knit. Insert left-hand needle into front of these stitches and knit them together

Central Double Dec
Slip first and second stitches together as if to knit. Knit 1 stitch. Pass two slipped stitches over the knit stitch.

PLUM LOTUS DISHCLOTH

by Kalurah Hudson

A simple seed stitch borders this pretty lace dishcloth. Slip stitch mock cables separate the delicate lotus shapes. Using a yarn like the super soft Comfy Worsted, this pattern is also perfect for a lovely facecloth. Pattern is both written and charted.

FINISHED MEASUREMENTS

11.25" high X 10.75" wide, blocked

YARN

Knit Picks Comfy Worsted (75% Pima Cotton, 25% Acrylic; 109 yards/50g): Vinca 25320, 1 ball

NEEDLES

US 6 (4mm) straight or 24" circular needles, or size to obtain gauge

NOTIONS

Yarn Needle

GAUGE

16 sts and 24 rows = 4" in Seed st, blocked

Notes:

Sl1, K2, PSSO: Sl1 K-wise, K next 2 sts, pass Sl st over 2 K sts. (3 sts decreased to 2.)

Sl1, M1, K2, PSSO: Sl1 K-wise, using tip of right hand needle lift the right strand of st below this st (from right to left) and place it on left hand needle, K this st, K next 2 sts, pass Sl st over 3 K sts.

Sl1, KFB, K1, PSSO: Sl1 K-wise, KFB, K1, pass Sl st over 3 K sts.
Make Bobble (MB): (K1, YO, K1, YO, K1) in the same st, drop all sts from left hand needle, turn, K5, turn, K5, pass second st on right hand needle over first st 4 times. 1 st left on right hand needle. Place this st P-wise back onto left hand needle and K it. Bobble is now on right hand needle and completed.

Sl1, K2tog, PSSO: Sl1, K2tog, pass Sl st over. (3 sts decreased to 1.)

Plum Lotus Chart (worked flat over 43 sts)
Rows 1 - 8: (P1, K1) to last st, P1.
Row 9 (WS): [(P1, K1) x 4, K2] twice, (P1, K1) twice, K2, (P1, K1) x 4, K2, P1, (K1, P1) x 3.
Row 10: (P1, K1) twice, P1, K2, P3, YO, SSK, K3, K2tog, YO, P3, Sl1 K-wise, K2, PSSO, P3, YO, SSK, K3, K2tog, YO, P3, K2, (P1, K1) twice, P1.
Row 11: (P1, K1) twice, P3, K4, P5, K4, P1, YO, P1, K4, P5, K4, P3, (K1, P1) twice.
Row 12: (P1, K1) twice, P1, K2, P4, YO, SSK, K1 K2tog, YO, P4, K3, P4, YO, SSK, K1, K2tog, YO, P4, K2, (P1, K1) twice, P1.
Row 13: (P1, K1) twice, P3, K5, P4, K4, (P3, K5) twice, P3, (K1, P1) twice.
Row 14: (P1, K1) twice, P1, K2, P5, YO, Sl1, K2tog, PSSO, YO, P5, Sl1, M1, K2, PSSO, P5, YO, Sl1, K2tog, PSSO, YO, P5, K2, (P1, K1) twice, P1.
Row 15: (P1, K1) twice, (P3, K13) twice, P3, (K1, P1) twice.
Row 16: (P1, K1) twice, P1, (K1 YO, SSK, P11, K2tog, YO) twice, (K1, P1) x 3.
Row 17: (P1, K1) twice, P4, K11, P5, K11, P4, (K1, P1) twice.
Row 18: P1, (K1, P1) twice, (K1, YO, K1, SSK, P4, MB, P4, K2tog, K1, YO) twice, (K1, P1) x 3.
Row 19: (P1, K1) twice, P5, K9, P7, K9, P5, (K1, P1) twice.
Row 20: (P1, K1) twice, P1, (K1, YO, K2, SSK, P2, MB, P1, MB, P2, K2tog, K2, YO) twice, (K1, P1) x 3.
Row 21: (P1, K1) twice, P6, K7, P9, K7, P6, (K1, P1) twice.
Row 22: (P1, K1) twice, P1, (K1, YO, K3, SSK, P2, MB, P2, K2tog, K3, YO) twice, (K1, P1) x 3.
Row 23: (P1, K1) twice, P7, K5, P11, K5, P7, (K1, P1) twice.
Row 24: (P1, K1) twice, P1, (K1, YO, K4, SSK, P3, K2tog, K4, YO) twice, (K1, P1) x 3.
Row 25: (P1, K1) twice, P8, K3, P13, K3, P8, (K1, P1) twice.
Row 26: (P1, K1) twice, P1, (K1 YO, K5, SSK, P1, K2tog, K5, YO) twice, (K1, P1) x 3.
Row 27: (P1, K1) twice, P9, K1 P15, K1, P9, (K1, P1) twice.
Row 28: (P1, K1) twice, P1, (K1, YO, K2, K2tog, YO, SSK, K1, P1, K1, K2tog, YO, SSK, K2, YO) twice, (K1, P1) x 3.
Row 29: (P1, K1) twice, P6, (K1, P2) twice, K1, P9, (K1, P2) twice, K1, P6, (K1, P1) twice.
Row 30: (P1, K1) twice, P1, K3, K2tog, YO, P1, YO, SSK, P1, K2tog, YO, P1, YO, SSK, K5, K2tog, YO, P1, YO, SSK, P1, K2tog, YO, P1, YO, SSK, K3, (P1, K1) twice, P1.
Row 31: (P1, K1) twice, P5, K3, P3, K3, P7, K3, P3, K3, P5, (K1, P1) twice.
Row 32: (P1, K1) twice, P1, K2, K2tog, YO, P3, Sl1 K-wise, K2, PSSO, P3, YO, SSK, K3, K2tog, YO, P3, Sl1 K-wise, K2, PSSO, P3, YO, SSK, K2, (P1, K1) twice, P1.
Row 33: (P1, K1) twice, P4, K4, P1, YO, P1, K4, P5, K4, P1, YO, P1, K4, P4, (K1, P1) twice.
Row 34: (P1, K1) twice, P1, (K1, K2tog, YO, P4, K3, P4, YO, SSK) twice, (K1, P1) x 3.
Row 35: (P1, K1) twice, (P3, K5) x 4, P3, (K1, P1) twice.
Row 36: (P1, K1) twice, P1, K2tog, YO, P5, Sl1, M1, K2, PSSO, P5, YO, Sl1, K2tog, PSSO, YO, P5, Sl1, M1, K2, PSSO, P5, YO, SSK, (P1, K1) twice, P1.
Row 37: (P1, K1) twice, P1, K7, P3, K13, P3, K7, (P1, K1) twice, P1.
Row 38: (P1, K1) twice, P7, K2tog, YO, K1, YO, SSK, P11, K2tog, YO, K1 YO, SSK, P7, (K1, P1) twice.
Row 39: (P1, K1) twice, P1, K6, P5, K11, P5, K6, (P1, K1) twice, P1.
Row 40: (P1, K1) twice, P1, (MB, P4, K2tog, (K1, YO) twice, K1, SSK, P4) twice, MB, (P1, K1) twice, P1.
Row 41: (P1, K1) twice, P1, K5, P7, K9, P7, K5, (P1, K1) twice, P1.
Row 42: (P1, K1) twice, P2, MB, P2, K2tog, K2, YO, K1, YO, K2, SSK, P2, MB, P1, MB, P2, K2tog, K2, YO, K1 YO, K2, SSK, P2, MB, P2, (K1, P1) twice.
Row 43: (P1, K1) twice, P1, K4, P9, K7, P9, K4, (P1, K1) twice, P1.
Row 44: (P1, K1) twice, P1, (MB, P2, K2tog, K3, YO, K1 YO, K3, SSK, P2) twice, MB, (P1, K1) twice, P1.
Row 45: (P1, K1) twice, P1, K3, P11, K5, P11, K3, (P1, K1) twice, P1.
Row 46: (P1, K1) twice, (P3, K2tog, K4, YO, K1, YO, K4, SSK) twice, P3, (K1, P1) twice.

Row 47: (P1, K1) twice, P1, K2, P13, K3, P13, K2, (P1, K1) twice, P1.
Row 48: (P1, K1) twice, P2, K2tog, K5, YO, K1, YO, K5, SSK, P1, K2tog, K5, YO, K1 YO, K5, SSK, P2, (K1, P1) twice.
Row 49: (P1, K1) x 3, P15, K1, P15, (K1, P1) x 3.
Row 50: (P1, K1) twice, P2, K1, K2tog, YO, SSK, K2, YO, K1 YO, K2, K2tog, YO, SSK, K1, P1, K1, K2tog, YO, SSK, K2, YO, K1, YO, K2, K2tog, YO, SSK, K1, P2, (K1, P1) twice.
Row 51: (P1, K1) twice, P1, (K1, P2, K1, P9, K1, P2) twice, (K1, P1) x 3.
Row 52: (P1, K1) twice, P2, K2tog, YO, P1, YO, SSK, K5, K2tog, YO, P1, YO, SSK, P1, K2tog, YO, P1, YO, SSK, K5, K2tog, YO, P1, YO, SSK, P2, (K1, P1) twice.
Row 53: (P1, K1) twice, P1, K5, P7, K3, P3, K3, P7, K5, (P1, K1) twice, P1.
Row 54: (P1, K1) twice, P6, YO, SSK, K3, K2tog, YO, P3, Sl1 K-wise, K2, PSSO, P3, YO, SSK, K3, K2tog, YO, P6, (K1, P1) twice.
Row 55: (P1, K1) twice, P1, K6, P5, K4, P1, YO, P1, K4, P5, K6, (P1, K1) twice, P1.
Row 56: (P1, K1) twice, P7, YO, SSK, K1, K2tog, YO, P4, K3, P4, YO, SSK, K1, K2tog, YO, P7, (K1, P1) twice.
Row 57: (P1, K1) twice, P1, K7, P3, K5, P3, K5, P3, K7, (P1, K1) twice, P1.
Row 58: (P1, K1) twice, P8, YO, Sl1, K2tog, PSSO, YO, P5, Sl1, KFB, K1, PSSO, P5, YO, Sl1, K2tog, PSSO, YO, P8, (K1, P1) twice.
Rows 59 - 67: (P1, K1) to last st, P1.

DIRECTIONS

CO 43 sts. Work Rows 1-67 of the Chart, following either the written or charted instructions. Read the Chart RS rows (even numbers) from right to left, and WS rows (odd numbers) from left to right.
BO on RS in Seed St pattern.

Finishing

Weave in ends, wash and block to finished measurements.

Legend

knit
RS: knit stitch
WS: purl stitch

purl
RS: purl stitch
WS: knit stitch

yo
Yarn Over

ssk
Slip one stitch as if to knit, slip another stitch as if to knit. Insert left-hand needle into front of these 2 stitches and knit them together.

k2tog
Knit two stitches together as one stitch

sl1, k2, psso
Sl1 K-wise, K next 2 sts, pass Sl st over 2 K sts. (3 sts decreased to 2.)

sl1 k2tog psso
slip 1, k2tog, pass slip stitch over k2tog

sl1, m1, k2, psso
Sl1 K-wise, using tip of right-hand needle lift the right strand of st below this st (from right to left) and place it on left-hand needle, K this st, K next 2 sts, pass Sl st over 3 K sts.

sl1, kfb, k1, psso
Sl1 K-wise, KFB, K1, pass Sl st over 3 K sts.

bobble
(k1, yo, k1, yo, k1) in the same st, drop all sts from left-hand needle, turn, k5, turn, k5, pass second st on right-hand needle over first st 4 times. 1 st left on right-hand needle. Place this st p-wise back onto left-hand needle and K it. Bobble is now on the right-hand needle and completed.

Plum Lotus Chart

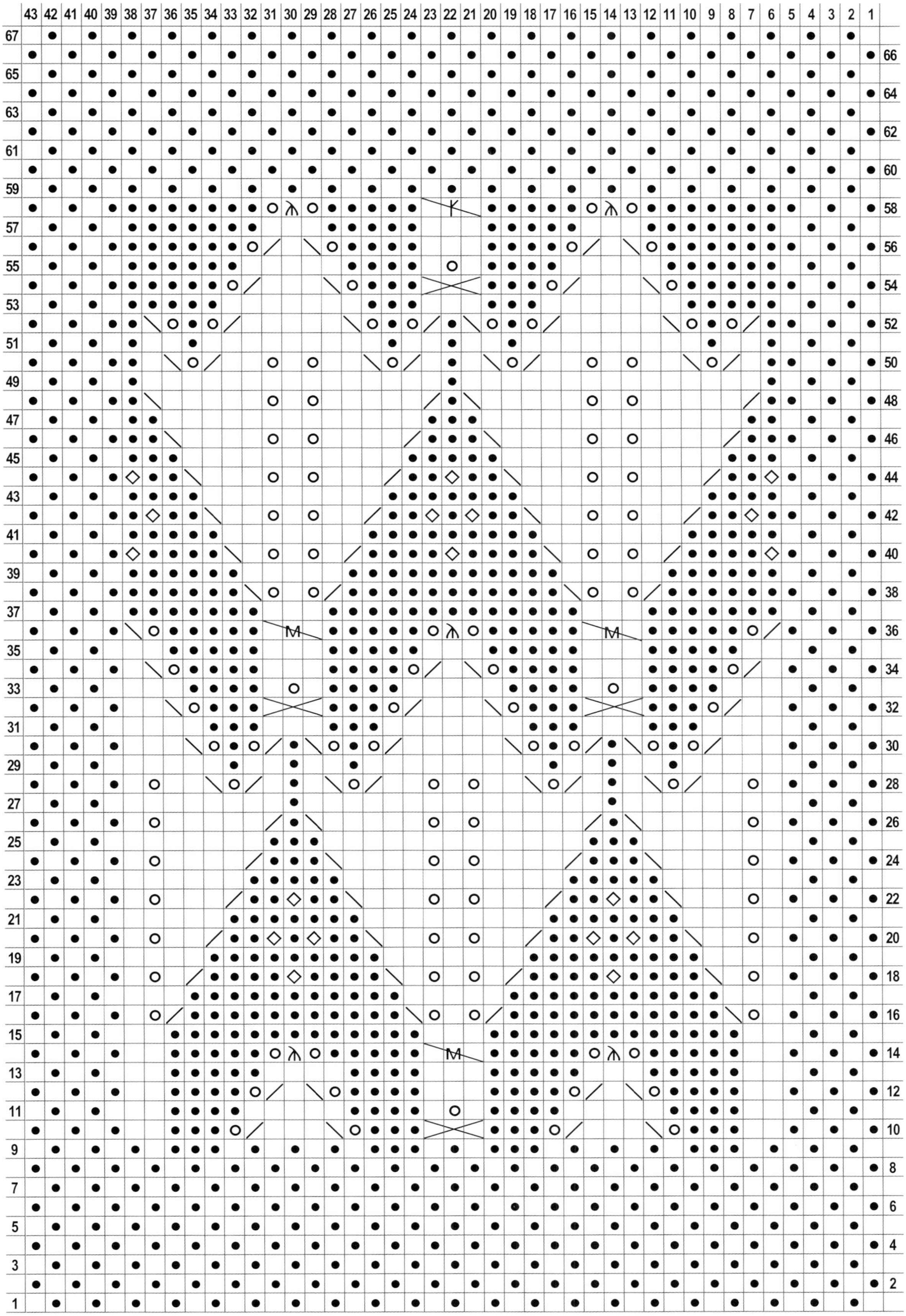

KNOTTED CABLES WASHCLOTH

by Kendra Nitta

The cables on this lovely washcloth look complicated, but are well-suited to adventurous beginners eager to expand their knitting skills. The increases and decreases in the garter stitch rows help keep the top and bottom from flaring.

FINISHED MEASUREMENTS

8.5" wide x 7.25" high, blocked

YARN

Knit Picks Dishie (100% Cotton; 190 yards/100g): Mint 27041, 1 ball

NEEDLES

US 7 (4.5mm) straight or circular needles, or size to obtain gauge

NOTIONS

Cable needle

GAUGE

20 sts and 36 rows = 4" in garter st, unblocked. (Gauge for this project is approximate)

Notes:

Cable pattern is both written and charted. If using the chart, read the charts RS rows (odd numbers) from right to left, and WS rows (even numbers) from left to right.

2/2 RC

Sl2 to CN, hold to back, K2; K2 from CN.

2/2 LC

Sl2 to CN, hold to front, K2; K2 from CN.

Cable Chart (worked flat over 54 sts)

Rows 1 (RS): K5, P2, (2/2 RC) 3 times, P2, K12, P2, (2/2 RC) 3 times, P2, K5.

Rows 2, 4, 6, 8, 10, 12, 14, 16, 18, and 20 (WS): K7, (P12, K2) twice, P12, K7.

Row 3: K5, P2, K2, (2/2 LC) twice, K2, P2, K12, P2, K2, (2/2 LC) twice, K2, P2, K5.

Row 5: Repeat Row 1.

Row 7: Repeat Row 3.

Row 9: Repeat Row 1.

Row 11: K5, P2, K12, P2, (2/2 RC) 3 times, P2, K12, P2, K5.

Row 13: K5, P2, K12, P2, K2, (2/2 LC) twice), K2, P2, K12, P2, K5.

Row 15: Repeat Row 11.

Row 17: Repeat Row 13.

Row 19: Repeat Row 11.

DIRECTIONS

CO 42 sts. Knit 2 rows.

Next Row: K10, KFB, K20, KFB, K10. 44 sts.

Knit one row.

Next Row: K8, KFB, K3, KFB, K18, KFB, K3, KFB, K8. 48 sts.

Knit one row.

Next Row: K7, KFB, (K3, KFB) twice, K16, KFB, (K3, KFB) twice, K7. 54 sts.

Knit one row.

Begin Cable Chart. Work Rows 1-20 twice, then Rows 1-9 once more. Knit one row.

Next Row (RS): K7, K2tog, (K3, K2tog) twice, K16, K2tog, (K3, K2tog) twice, K7. 48 sts.

Knit one row.

Next Row: K8, K2tog, K3, K2Tog, K18, K2tog, K3, K2tog, K8. 44 sts.

Knit one row.

Next Row: K10, K2tog, K20, K2tog, K10. 42 sts.

Knit two rows. BO.

Finishing

Weave in ends, wash and block to finished dimensions.

Knotted Cables Chart

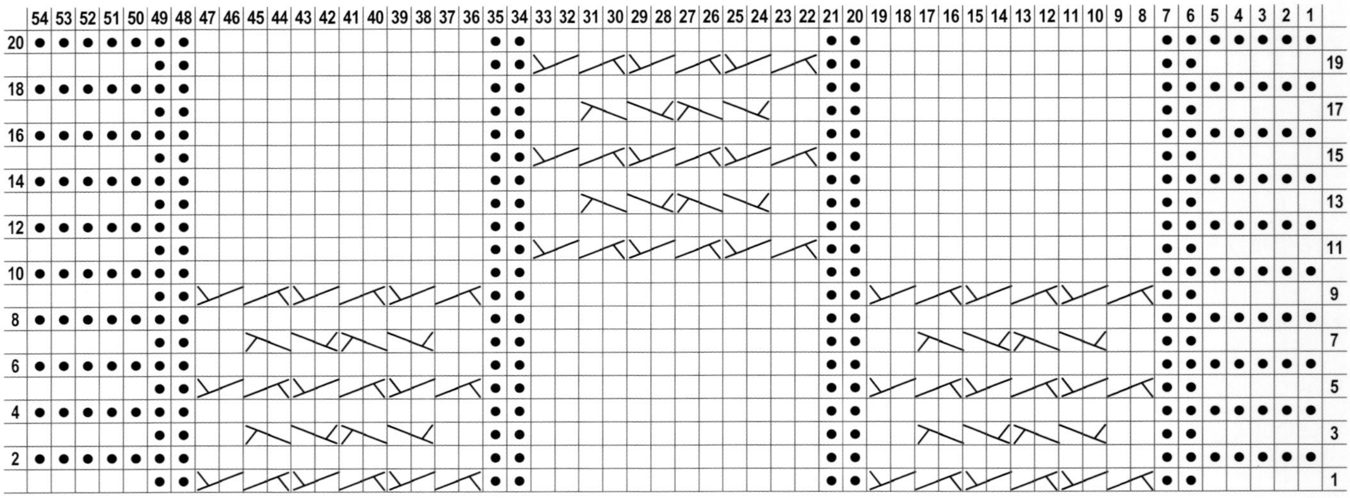

Legend

knit
RS: knit
WS: purl

purl
RS: purl
WS: knit

2/2 RC
sl2 to CN, hold in back. k2, k2 from CN

2/2 LC
sl 2 to CN, hold in front. k2, k2 from CN

SUMMER

Summer afternoon, summer afternoon; to me those have always been the two most beautiful words in the English language.

- Henry James

CHECKERBOARD DISHCLOTH

by Allison Griffith

This reversible washcloth is knit from the bottom up in a single piece. A garter stitch border is worked around the edge of a panel of a charted pattern of knits and purls.

FINISHED MEASUREMENTS

8.25" x 8"

YARN

Knit Picks Dishie (100% Cotton; 190 yards/100g): Begonia 25790, 1 ball

NEEDLES

US 8 (4.5mm) straight or 24" or longer circular needles, or size to obtain gauge

NOTIONS

Yarn Needle

GAUGE

19 sts and 28 rows = 4" over Checkerboard pattern, blocked lightly

Notes:

This pattern is charted.

Garter Stitch (worked flat over any number of sts)

All Rows: K.

When working charts back and forth, read the chart RS rows (odd numbers) from right to left, and WS rows (even numbers) from left to right.

DIRECTIONS

Loosely CO 39 sts.

Work 4 rows in Garter st.

Work Checkerboard Chart across, repeating pattern repeat 3 times. Work rows 1-14 three times, then work rows 1-7.

Work 4 rows in Garter st.

BO loosely.

Finishing

Weave in ends, and block lightly.

Checkerboard Chart

	19	18	17	16	15	14	13	12	11	10	9	8	7	6	5	4	3	2	1	
14	●	●						●		●		●						●	●	
									●		●									13
12	●	●						●		●		●						●	●	
									●		●									11
10	●	●						●		●		●						●	●	
									●		●									9
8	●	●						●		●		●						●	●	
			●		●		●						●		●		●			7
6	●	●		●		●								●		●		●	●	
			●		●		●						●		●		●			5
4	●	●		●		●								●		●		●	●	
			●		●		●						●		●		●			3
2	●	●		●		●								●		●		●	●	
			●		●		●						●		●		●			1

Legend

☐ knit
RS: knit stitch
WS: purl stitch

● purl
RS: purl stitch
WS: knit stitch

Pattern Repeat

MIXED BERRY DISHCLOTH

by Allison Griffith

Celebrate berry season with this sweet 2 color dishcloth! Using berrylicious colors, this dishcloth is knit from the bottom up in a single piece. A garter stitch border gives way to a panel of textured stitches featuring slipped stitches to create a beautiful and colorful dishcloth. Carrying the unused color up the sides gives it a neat edge and saves you from working in additional ends.

FINISHED MEASUREMENTS

7" square

YARN

Knit Picks Dishie (100% Cotton; 190 yards/100g): C1 Begonia 25790, C2 Mulberry 25784, 1 ball each

NEEDLES

US 8 (4.5mm) straight or circular needles, or size to obtain gauge

NOTIONS

Yarn Needle

GAUGE

16 sts and 32 rows = 4" over Mixed Berry pattern, blocked lightly

Notes:

Every 4th row, switch colors without breaking yarn. Wrap inactive yarn around working yarn along the right edge as you go to create a neat edge.

Read the charts RS rows (odd numbers) from right to left, and WS rows (even numbers) from left to right.

DIRECTIONS

With C2, CO 28 sts.

K 3 rows.

Next Row (WS): K2, (M1, K3) 8 times, M1, K2. (37 sts)

Work Rows 1-8 of Mixed Berry Chart 6 times, then Rows 1-4 once more, repeating pattern repeat (columns 4-7) 8 times across.

Break C1.

Next Row (RS): With C2, K2, (K2tog, K2) 8 times, K2tog, K1.

(28 sts)

K 3 rows.

BO loosely.

Finishing

Weave in ends, and block lightly.

Mixed Berry Chart

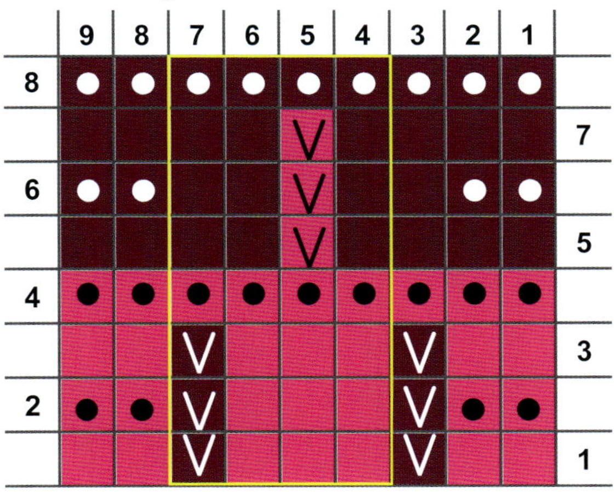

Legend

knit
RS: knit stitch
WS: purl stitch

slip
RS: Slip stitch as if to knit, holding yarn in back
WS: Slip stitch as if to purl, holding yarn in front

purl
RS: purl stitch
WS: knit stitch

C1 - Begonia

C2 - Mulberry

Pattern Repeat

TROPICAL COLORBLOCK DISHCLOTH

by Ann Weaver

Bring a bit of the color to your kitchen! Knit in one piece, this fun pattern uses garter stitch for a completely reversible piece. After completing the first section, the dishcloth is turned 90 degrees to pick up stitches for the second. It's perfect for beginner knitters looking for some practice as well as for seasoned veterans looking for a relaxing project. Mix and match your favorite colors this will be project you'll turn to again and again.

FINISHED MEASUREMENTS

Approximately 9x9", washed

YARN

Knit Picks Dishie (100% Cotton; 190 yards/100g): C1 Begonia 25790; C2 Clementine 25403; C3 Fiesta Red 25786; 1 ball each

NEEDLES

US 7 (4.5mm) straight or circular needles, or size to obtain gauge

NOTIONS

Yarn Needle

GAUGE

18 sts and 34 rows = 4" in Garter st, washed

Notes:

This dishcloth is worked in one piece. Stitches from the edge of the first section are picked up to knit the second section.

DIRECTIONS

Using C1, CO 25 sts.

K 50 rows.

Cut C1 and join C2.

Using C2, K 28 rows.

BO loosely.

Turn work clockwise 90 degrees. Using C3, PU and K39 sts along edge of work.

K 28 rows.

BO loosely.

Finishing

Weave in ends, wash, and enjoy!

CHEVRON STRIPES DISHCLOTH

by Ann Weaver

Create a striking dishcloth with this fun pattern. Using a simple chevron stitch and blocks of color, this project works up quickly and can easily be customized to your match your kitchen.

FINISHED MEASUREMENTS

10.75" wide x 11.5" high, blocked

YARN

Knit Picks Dishie (100% Cotton; 190 yards/100g): C1 Kenai 25788; C2 Clementine 25403; C3 Jalapeno 25785; 1 ball each

NEEDLES

US 7 (4.5mm) straight or circular needles, or size to obtain gauge

NOTIONS

Yarn Needle
Stitch Markers

GAUGE

18 sts and 20 rows = 4" in Chevron Pattern, blocked

Notes:

Seed St Pattern (worked flat over even number of sts)
Row 1 (RS): (K1, P1) to end.
Row 2 (WS): (P1, K1) to end.
Rep Rows 1-2 for pattern.

Chevron Pattern (worked flat over 48 sts)
Row 1 (RS): K1, P1, K1, PM, (K2tog, K4, KFB twice, K4, SSK) 3 times, PM, P1, K1, P1.
Row 2 (WS): P1, K1, P1, SM, P to last 3 sts, SM, K1, P1, K1.
Rep Rows 1-2 for pattern, SM as you come to them.

DIRECTIONS

Using the Long-Tail CO and C1, CO 48 sts.
Work 4 rows of Seed st.
Work 10 rows in Chevron Pattern. You can cut C1 at this point or carry it up the side of your work.

Stripe Pattern
Using C2, work 4 rows in Chevron Pattern. Do not cut C2.
Using C3, work Row 1 of Chevron Pattern.

Next Row (WS): P1, K1, P1, SM, K to M, SM, P1, K1, P1.
Using C2, work 4 rows in Chevron Pattern. Cut C2.
Join C1 if you have not carried it up the side of your work.
Using C1, work 10 rows of Chevron Pattern.

Rep Stripe Pattern one more time.

Work 4 rows of Seed St.

BO.

Finishing

Weave in ends, block and enjoy!

KNITS AND PURLS DISHCLOTH

by Ann Weaver

Practice basic knitting and purling skills with this easy and fun dishcloth! A series of 5 stitch patterns weave up this project, resulting in a cute sampler that is as useful as it is attractive.

FINISHED MEASUREMENTS

11" square

YARN

Knit Picks Dishie (100% Cotton; 190 yards/100g): Jalapeno 25785, 1 ball.

NEEDLES

US 7 (4.5mm) straight or circular needles, or size to obtain gauge

NOTIONS

Yarn Needle

GAUGE

18 sts and 26 rows = 4" in Knits and Purls pattern, blocked.

Notes:

Read the charts RS rows (odd numbers) from right to left, and WS rows (even numbers) from left to right. This pattern is fully charted.

DIRECTIONS

Using the Long Tail Cast On Method, CO 50 sts.

Work Rows 1-70 of Knits and Purls Chart, repeating 10-stitch pattern 5 times across.

BO K-wise.

Finishing

Weave in ends, block and enjoy!

Knits and Purls Chart

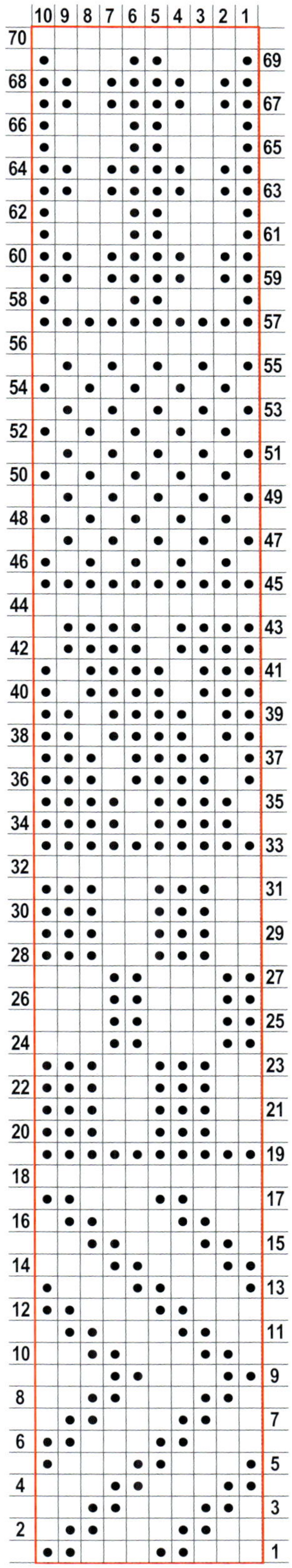

Legend

knit
RS: knit stitch
WS: purl stitch

purl
RS: purl stitch
WS: knit stitch

Pattern Repeat

BYZANTINE DISHCLOTH

by Erica Jackofsky

Inspired by a Byzantine motif, this dishcloth will add a bit of beauty to your kitchen. The patterning is formed by slipping stitches from the previous rows to carry color up, only one color is worked per row. Choose colors with good contrast to show the pattern to the fullest extent. Perfect for those new to colorwork, you'll have this project done in no time.

FINISHED MEASUREMENTS

Approximately 12 x 10"

YARN

Knit Picks Dishie (100% Cotton; 190 yards/100g): C1 Clarity 27037; C2 Begonia 25790, 1 ball each

NEEDLES

US 6 (4mm) straight or circular needles, or size to obtain gauge

NOTIONS

Yarn Needle

GAUGE

20 sts and 25 rows = 4" over Byzantine pattern, blocked. (Gauge for this project is approximate.)

Notes:

Throughout the pattern you will alternate between 2 rows of each color. Patterning is formed by slipping stitches from the previous rows to carry color up, only one color is worked per row.

Read the chart RS rows (odd numbers) from right to left, and WS rows (even numbers) from left to right.

DIRECTIONS

With C1, CO 59 sts.

Work Rows 1-66 of Byzantine Chart.

With C1, BO all sts.

Finishing

Weave in ends, wash and block as necessary.

Byzantine Chart

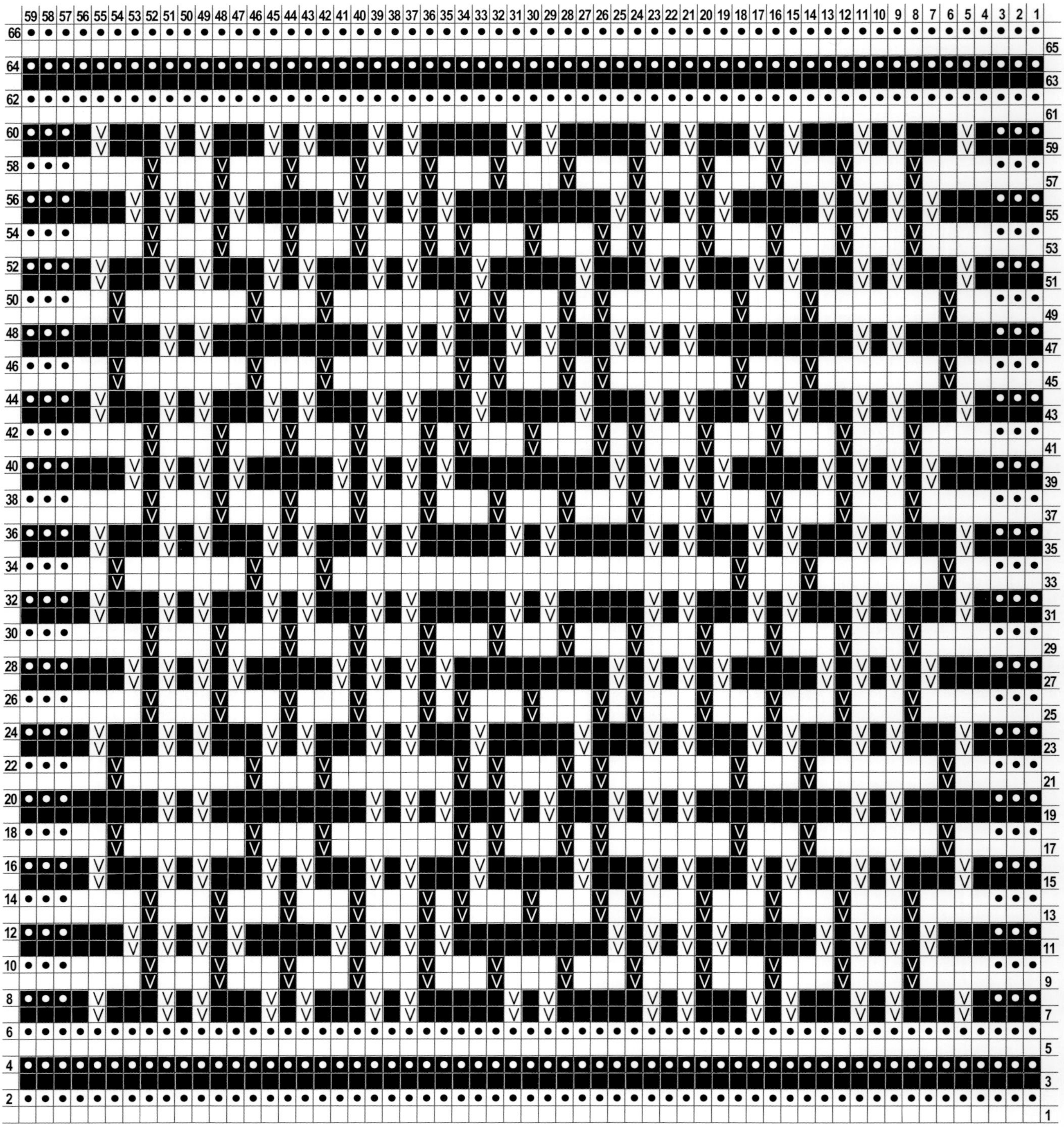

Legend

- ☐ **knit** RS: knit stitch WS: purl stitch
- ⊡ **purl** RS: purl stitch WS: knit stitch
- V **Slip Stitch** RS: slip stitch WYIB WS: slip stitch WYIF
- ☐ C1
- ■ C2

BERRY BASKET DISHCLOTH

by Faith Schmidt

Berry Basket Dishcloth is a quick and fun knit. The stitch pattern is easy to memorize, and becomes intuitive after working a few rows. It can easily be resized to fit your needs.

FINISHED MEASUREMENTS

Approximately 10.5" square, unblocked

YARN

Knit Picks Dishie (100% Cotton; 190 yards/100g): Coffee 25399, 1 ball

NEEDLES

US 7 (4.5mm) straight or circular needles, or size to obtain gauge

NOTIONS

Yarn Needle

GAUGE

18 sts and 29 rows = 4" over Berry Basket stitch, unblocked. Exact gauge is not important to this project.

Notes:

To resize, cast on a multiple of 6 plus 2 sts, and knit to desired length.

Berry Basket Stitch Pattern (worked flat over multiple of 6 plus 2 sts)

Rows 1 and 3(RS): K2, *P4, K2; repeat from * to end of row.

Rows 2 and 4 (WS): *P2, K4; repeat from * to last 2 sts, P2.

Row 5: K.

Row 6: P.

Rows 7 and 9: P2, *P1, K2, P3; repeat from * to end of row.

Rows 8 and 10: *K3, P2, K1; repeat from * to last 2 sts, K2.

Row 11: K.

Row 12: P.

Rep Rows 1-12 for pattern.

DIRECTIONS

CO 50 sts, using the Long Tail Cast-on.

Work Berry Basket Pattern (Rows 1-12) 6 times total, then work Rows 1-3 once.

BO k-wise on WS.

Finishing

Weave in ends. Block if desired.

WOVEN DISHCLOTH

by Faith Schmidt

The Woven Dishcloth is a quick and fun knit. Binding off stitches, and then casting them on again in the next row creates the stitch pattern. It can easily be resized to fit your needs

FINISHED MEASUREMENTS
8.5" wide x 9.5" tall, unblocked

YARN
Knit Picks Dishie (100% Cotton; 190 yards/100g): Azure 25412, 1 ball.

NEEDLES
US 5 (3.75mm) straight or circular needles, or size to obtain gauge

NOTIONS
Yarn Needle

GAUGE
22 sts and 26 rows = 4" over Woven Stitch, unblocked. (Exact gauge is not important to this project.)

Notes:
When working the Woven Pattern stitch, BO P-wise. To bind off there need to be two sts to work with, so after purling the first st, purl two more sts, then lift the second st from the end of the right needle over the first st and off the needle. Continue binding off until reaching the end of the P sts in that repeat. There will be the first stitch purled, a gap, and the then the last bound off st before the K sts.

For Rows 6 and 16, use the Backwards Loop CO.

When working Rows 7 and 17 (the rows immediately after the cast on rows), P the last 2 sts of the newly cast on sts TBL. This will tighten the sts up and give the holes a cleaner look.

Woven Pattern (worked flat over multiple of 10 plus 7 sts)
Rows 1 and 3 (RS): *P7, K3; repeat from * to last 7 sts, P7.
Rows 2 and 4 (WS): *K7, P3; repeat from * to last 7 sts, K7.
Row 5: *P1, BO 5 sts P-wise, K3, repeat from * last 7 sts, P1, BO 5 sts.
Row 6: *K1, CO 5 using the Backward Loop CO, K1, P3; repeat from * to last 7 sts, K1, CO 5, K1.
Row 7: *P4, P2 TBL, P1, K3; repeat from * to last 7 sts, P4, P2 TBL, P1
Row 9: Same as Row 1.
Rows 8 and 10: Same as Row 2.
Rows 11 and 13: P2, *K3, P7; repeat from * to last 5 sts, K3, P2.
Rows 12 and 14: K2, *P3, K7; repeat from * to last 5 sts, P3, K2.
Row 15: P2, *K3, P1, BO 5 sts; repeat from * to last 5 sts, K3, P2.
Row 16: K2, *P3, K1, CO 5 using the Backward Loop CO, K1; repeat from * to last 5 sts, P3, K2.
Row 17: P2, *K3, P4, P2 TBL, P1; repeat from * to last 5 sts, K3, P2.
Row 19: Same as Row 11.
Rows 18 and 20: Same as Row 12.
To resize, CO a multiple of 10 plus 7 sts, and work to desired length, ending with either Row 9 or 19.

DIRECTIONS
CO 47 sts, using the Long Tail Cast-on.

Work Rows 1-20 of Woven Pattern 3 times total. On the last repeat, end with Row 19. BO K-wise.

Finishing
Weave in ends. Block if desired.

GEMOLOGY DISHCLOTH

by Joyce Fassbender

This richly textured dishcloth is wonderful for washing. Using simple knits and purls, the eye catching center is surrounded by a garter border. Knit it in a super soft yarn like Shine Worsted and it'll be the perfect companion for your bath.

FINISHED MEASUREMENTS

8.75" wide x 6.25" high

YARN

Knit Picks Shine Worsted (60% Pima Cotton, 40% Modal; 75 yards/50g): Serrano 24496, 1 ball

NEEDLES

US 7 (4.5mm) straight or circular needles, or size to obtain gauge

NOTIONS

Yarn Needle

GAUGE

18 sts and 24 rows = 4" in St st, blocked

Notes:
This pattern is fuly written out and not charted. The cloth has a textured center surrounded by a garter stitch edge.

Garter St (worked flat)
All Rows: K.

DIRECTIONS

CO 39 sts using Long Tail CO.
K 3 rows in Garter st.

Body

Work Rows 1-16 twice.
Row 1 (WS): K11, (P2, K1) five times, P2, K11.
Row 2 (RS): K3, P7, (K2, P1) twice, K2, P3, (K2, P1) twice, K2, P7, K3.
Row 3: K9, (P2, K1) twice, P2, K5, (P2, K1) twice, P2, K9.
Row 4: K3, P5, (K2, P1) twice, K2, P3, K1, P3, (K2, P1) twice, K2, P5, K3.
Row 5: K7, (P2, K1) twice, P2, K3, P3, K3, (P2, K1) twice, P2, K7.
Row 6: K3, P3, (K2, P1) twice, K2, P3, K5, P3, (K2, P1) twice, K2, P3, K3.
Row 7: K5, (P2, K1) twice, P2, K3, P3, K1, P3, K3, (P2, K1) twice, P2, K5.
Row 8: K3, (P1, K2) three times, (P3, K3) twice, P3, (K2, P1) three times, K3.
Row 9: K3, (P2, K1) twice, P2, K3, P3, K5, P3, K3, (P2, K1) twice, P2, K3.
Row 10: Rep Row 8.
Row 11: Rep Row 7.
Row 12: Rep Row 6.
Row 13: Rep Row 5.
Row 14: Rep Row 4.
Row 15: Rep Row 3.
Row 16: Rep Row 2.
Ending Rows
Row 1: K11, (P2, K1) five times, P2, K11.
K 5 rows in Garter st.

Finishing

BO all sts. Weave in ends, wash and block.

SEA SWELLS DISHCLOTH

by Joyce Fassbender

Have an adventure on the high seas without leaving your home! The Sea Swells Dishcloth uses a texture and lace pattern to create the rise and fall of ocean waves. The pattern is fully written and knits up quickly for a perfect piece to celebrate your love of the briny deep.

FINISHED MEASUREMENTS

7.75" wide x 8" high

YARN

Knit Picks Dishie (100% Cotton; 190 yards/100g): Kenai 25788, 1 ball

NEEDLES

US 7 (4.5mm) straight or circular needles, or size to obtain gauge

NOTIONS

Yarn Needle

GAUGE

18 sts and 24 rows = 4" in Sea Swell pattern, blocked

Notes:

The cloth has a textured lace center surrounded by a garter stitch edge.

Garter St

All Rows: K.

DIRECTIONS

CO 35 stitches using the Long Tail CO method.

Work 7 rows in Garter st.

Body

Row 1 (RS): (K4, YO, K3, K2tog) three times, K8.

Rows 2, 4, 6 & 8 (WS): K8, (P5, K4) three times.

Row 3: (K5, YO, K2, K2tog) three times, K8.

Row 5: (K6, YO, K1, K2tog) three times, K8.

Row 7: (K7, YO, K2tog) three times, K8.

Row 9: K8, (SSK, K3, YO, K4) three times.

Rows 10, 12, 14 & 16: (K4, P5) three times, K8.

Row 11: K8, (SSK, K2, YO, K5) three times.

Row 13: K8, (SSK, K1, YO, K6) three times.

Row 15: K8, (SSK, YO, K7) three times.

Repeat Rows 1-16 once, then Rows 1-8 once more.

Work 8 rows in Garter st.

Finishing

BO all stitches. Weave in ends, wash and block.

FALL

Autumn is a second spring when every leaf is a flower.

- Albert Camus

CAT FACE DISHCLOTH

by Allyson Dykhuizen

Me-wow! This sweet dishcloth is perfect for all cat lovers. Working from the center out, this fast and fun dishcloth is knit in the round, with whiskers and nose added with duplicate stitch. Picking up stitches for the ears completes this cute kitty and will be a delightful addition to your kitchen!

FINISHED MEASUREMENTS
7.5" across not including ears

YARN
Knit Picks CotLin DK (70% Tanguis Cotton, 30% Linen; 123 yards/50g): C1 Swan 24134, C2 Black 24468, 1 ball each

NEEDLES
US 5 (3.75mm) DPNs, or size to obtain gauge

NOTIONS
Yarn Needle
Removable Stitch Markers

GAUGE
22 sts and 36 Rnds = 4" in Garter St, blocked

DIRECTIONS

Face

With C2 CO 6 sts. Divide sts evenly between 3 DPNs. PM and join to work in the round.

Rnd 1: K.
Rnd 2: KFB around. 12 sts.
Rnd 3: Change to C1, K all sts.
Rnd 4: [K1, KFB] around. 18 sts.
Rnd 5: P6, (K1, P1) 3 times, (P1, K1) 3 times.
Rnd 6: [K2, KFB] around. 24 sts.
Rnd 7: P8, (K1, P1) 3 times, P4, (K1, P1) 3 times.
Rnd 8: [K3, KFB] around. 30 sts.
Rnd 9: P10, (K1, P1) 3 times, P7, (K1, P1) 3 times, P1.
Rnd 10: [K4, KFB] around. 36 sts.
Rnd 11: P12, (K1, P1) 3 times, P10, (K1, P1) 3 times, P2.
Rnd 12: [K5, KFB] around. 42 sts.
Rnd 13: P14, (K1, P1) 3 times, P13, (K1, P1) 3 times, P3.
Rnd 14: [K6, KFB] around. 48 sts.
Rnd 15: P16, (K1, P1) 3 times, P16, (K1, P1) 3 times, P4.
Rnd 16: [K7, KFB] around. 54 sts.
Rnd 17 and all odd rnds through 33: P.
Rnd 18: [K8, KFB] around.60 sts.
Rnd 20: [K9, KFB] around. 66 sts.
Rnd 22: [K10, KFB] around. 72 sts.
Rnd 24: [K11, KFB] around. 78 sts.
Rnd 26: [K12, KFB] around. 84 sts.
Rnd 28: [K13, KFB] around. 90 sts.
Rnd 30: [K14, KFB] around. 96 sts.
Rnd 32: [K15, KFB] around. 102 sts.
Rnd 33: P.
BO all sts.

Whiskers

With C2 thread your yarn needle and bring it up through the bottom of the V at the base of the first St st Whisker stripe. Go back through the fabric at the top right point of your V, then back up through the top left point. Go back through fabric at the bottom of the V to complete the duplicate st. Repeat this process for each of the 3 St st Whisker Stripe stitches. Two of the whisker stripes will be very clear on each side of the nose, while the third stripe will be broken up by increases. Do your best to make straight lines to match the other stripes.

Ears (make 2)

Lay your Cat Head dishcloth in front of you with the top of the head centered. Using your finished Whiskers as a reference, use removable st marker to mark top center of the head. Count over 6 sts from this point in both directions and place removable st markers. This marks the inside edges of both ears.

With C1 and RS facing, PU & K11, using the st markers as a reference. For the Left Ear, start picking up sts at the marker. For the Right Ear, count 11 sts to the left to determine where to start picking up sts.

Row 1 (WS): K2, P7, K2.
Row 2 (RS): K.
Rep last 2 rows 2 more times, then work Row 1 once more.
Row 8 (RS): K4, Sl2 sts tog, K1, PSSO, K4. 9 sts.
Row 9 (WS): K2, P5, K2.
Row 10: K3, Sl2 sts tog, K1, PSSO, K3. 7 sts.
Row 11: K2, P3, K2.
Row 12: K2, Sl2 sts tog, K1, PSSO, K2. 5 sts.
Row 13: K2, P1, K2.
Row 14: K1, Sl2 sts tog, K1, PSSO, K1. 3 sts.
Row 15: K1, P1, K1.
BO all sts.
With C2 work a duplicate st into all of the center St sts of each ear to fill the center of the ears completely.

Finishing

Weave in ends, wash and block to measurements.

INTRODUCTION TO INTARSIA DISHCLOTH

by Ann Weaver

Fascinated by the look of intarsia but don't know where to begin? Try this easy dishcloth for an easy introduction. Knit in garter stitch, colors change in the middle of the row for blocks of color without seaming. Simple & fun, choose your favorite colors and get ready to learn a new technique.

FINISHED MEASUREMENTS

11" Square

YARN

Knit Picks Dishie (100% Cotton; 190 yards/100g): C1 Azure 25412; C2 Ash 27040; 1 ball each

NEEDLES

US 7 (4.5mm) straight or circular needles, or size to obtain gauge

NOTIONS

Yarn Needle

GAUGE

18 sts and 30 rows = 4" in Garter stitch, blocked

Notes:

This dishcloth uses the Knitted Cast On. You can find a tutorial it here: http://tutorials.knitpicks.com/wptutorials/knitted-cast-on/. To work intarsia, whenever you change colors in the middle of a row, pick up the new color from under the working color to twist the yarns. This will prevent holes in your knitting at the color changes. Always twist the yarns behind your work. Because you are working in garter stitch, this means that you will have to bring the new color to the back of your work when you encounter it on each row.

You can find a tutorial for basic intarsia here: http://tutorials.knitpicks.com/wptutorials/intarsia/.

DIRECTIONS

Using the Knitted CO, with C1 CO 25 sts; with C2 CO 25 sts.

First section

Row 1 (RS): With C2, K25; with C1 K25.

Row 2 (WS): With C1, K25; with C2 K25.

Rep Rows 1-2 19 more times (40 rows worked total). Cut both yarns.

Second section

Row 1 (RS): Join C1 and K25; join C2 and K25.

Row 2 (WS): With C2, K25; with C1 K25.

Row 3: With C1, K25; with C2 K25.

Row 4: Rep Row 2.

Rep Rows 3-4 18 more times (40 rows worked total).

With C1, BO 25; with C2 BO 25.

Finishing

Weave in ends, block, and enjoy!

PICOT EDGE DISHCLOTH

by Ann Weaver

Picot love! This fun dishcloth will give you all the practice you need to create this sweet little decoration on any project. Entirely knit in one piece, you'll start with a variation of a Knitted Cast On and create your first row of picots, then continue them on every other row. Finally you'll get practice on a picot bind off. This dishcloth works up in a flash, and will be a charming addition to any kitchen!

FINISHED MEASUREMENTS

11" wide x 10" tall (including picots)

YARN

Knit Picks Dishie (100% Cotton; 190 yards/100g): Azure 25412, 1 ball.

NEEDLES

US 7 (4.5mm) straight or 24" circular needles or longer, or size to obtain gauge

NOTIONS

Yarn Needle

GAUGE

20 sts and 40 rows = 4" in Garter st, blocked

DIRECTIONS

Picot CO

The Picot CO incorporates the Knitted CO. You can find a tutorial here: http://tutorials.knitpicks.com/wptutorials/knitted-cast-on/.

Make a slipknot, leaving a 6-inch tail, CO 6 sts using the Knitted CO, BO 3 sts, Sl the st remaining on the right needle to the left needle P-wise. 4 sts.

*CO 6 sts using the Knitted CO, BO 3 sts, Sl the sts remaining on the right needle to the left needle P-wise. 3 sts inc.

Repeat from * 14 more times. —49 sts.

Body

Work Picot Edge Pattern for body of dishcloth as follows:

Rows 1 and 2: CO 3 sts using the Knitted CO, BO 3 sts, K to end.

Rows 3 and 4: K.

Repeat Rows 1-4 twenty one more times.

Picot BO.

*CO 3 sts using the Knitted CO, BO 6 sts (the 3 sts just CO and 3 more sts), Sl the st remaining on the right needle to the left needle P-wise; rep from * 15 more times.

Cut yarn and draw through last st.

Finishing

Weave in ends, block and enjoy!

DEER SEASON DISHCLOTH

by Ann Weaver

Whether you're in the woods or in the city, the Deer Season Dishcloth is sure to be a favorite. Knit completely in one color, the deer is added via duplicate stitch. It's the perfect project to decorate your lodge - or simply your kitchen.

FINISHED MEASUREMENTS

11.25x10", blocked

YARN

Knit Picks Dishie (100% Cotton; 190 yards/100g): MC Ash 27040; CC Clementine 25403; 1 ball each

NEEDLES

US 7 (4.5mm) straight or circular needles, or size to obtain gauge

NOTIONS

Yarn Needle

GAUGE

18 sts and 24 rows = 4" in St st, blocked

Notes:

Seed Stitch Edging (worked flat over multiple of 2 sts plus 1)

Every Row: (K1, P1) to last st, K1.

Duplicate St

The deer head is stitched onto this dishcloth using duplicate stitch. Here's a tutorial on this fun and easy technique: http://tutorials.knitpicks.com/wptutorials/embroidery-how-to-do-the-duplicate-stitch/

DIRECTIONS

Using MC, CO 51 sts.

Work 10 rows of Seed Stitch Edging.

Next Row (RS): (K1, P1) 2 times, K1, PM, K to last 5 sts, PM, (K1, P1) 2 times, K1.

Next Row (WS): (K1, P1) 2 times, K1, SM, P to last 5 sts, SM, (K1, P1) 2 times, K1.

Continue to work as established with 5 edge sts outside markers in Seed Stitch and center in St st until dishcloth measures 8.5" from CO edge.

Work 10 rows of Seed Stitch Edging.

BO all sts.

Deer Head

To set up for Duplicate Stitching the deer head, PM 13 sts in from each edge (5 edge sts plus 8 St st sts). The deer head will be stitched on the 25 sts between these markers. Begin stitching on the first row of St st above the Seed Stitch Edging.

Using CC, Duplicate St the deer head on your dishcloth following the Deer Head Chart.

Finishing

Weave in ends, wash, and enjoy!

Deer Head Chart

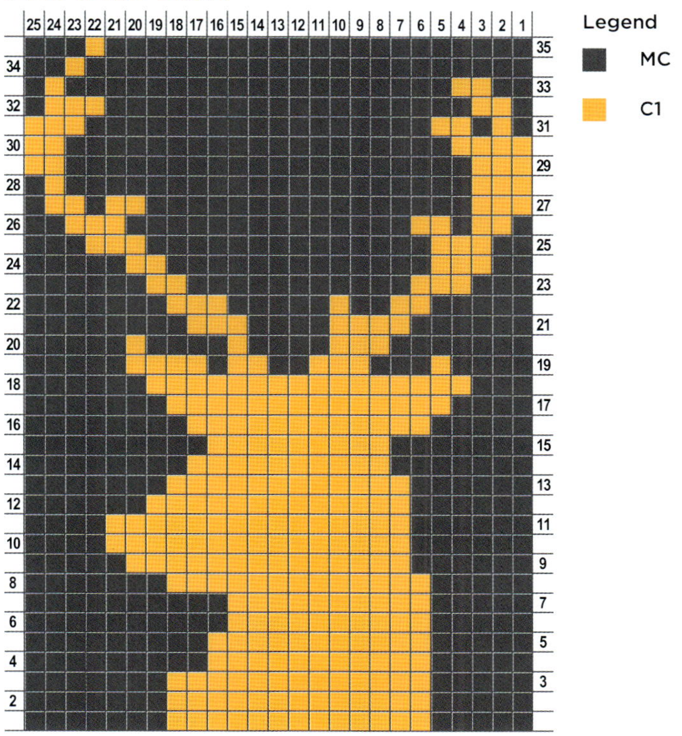

BULLSEYE DISHCLOTH

by Ann Weaver

Always hit your target with this fun dishcloth! Knit in the round from the inside out, the Bullseye Dishcloth is fast and fun project. The perfect gift for your favorite archery aficionado!

FINISHED MEASUREMENTS

10.25" circumference, blocked

YARN

Knit Picks Dishie (100% Cotton; 190 yards/100g): C1 Fiesta Red 25786; C2 Navy 26670; C3 Ash 27040; 1 ball each

NEEDLES

US 7 (4.5mm) DPNs, 16" and 24" circular needles, or size to obtain gauge

NOTIONS

Yarn Needle
Stitch Marker

GAUGE

18 sts and 34 rnds = 4" in Garter st in the rnd, blocked
18 sts and 23 rnds = 4" in St st in the rnd, blocked

Notes:
This dishcloth uses the Circular Cast On. You can find a tutorial for the Circular Cast On here: http://tutorials.knitpicks.com/wptutorials/circular-cast-on/

DIRECTIONS

With C1, CO 9 sts using the Circular CO and DPNs. Arrange the sts on three DPNs so there are 3 sts on each DPN. PM to indicate the beginning of the round, being careful not to twist sts.

Inc Rnd: (KFB) around.18 sts.

Section 1

Rnd 1: P.

Rnd 2: K.

Rnd 3: P.

Inc Rnd: (KFB) around. 36 sts

Section 2

Rnd 1: P.

Rnd 2: K.

Rep Rnds 1 & 2 twice more, then rep Rnd 1 once more. 7 rnds total.

Inc Rnd: (KFB) around. 72 sts

At this point, you likely will be able to transfer your sts from the DPNs to the 16" circular needle.

Section 3

Cut C1 and join C2.

Using C2, K 12 rnds.

Inc Rnd: (KFB) around. 144 sts.

At this point, you likely will be able to transfer your sts from the 16" circular needle to the 24" circular needle.

Section 4

Cut C2 and join C3.

Rnd 1: P.

Rnd 2: K.

Rep Rnds 1 & 2 three more times, then rep Rnd 1 once more.
9 rnds total.

BO loosely.

Finishing

Weave in ends, block, and enjoy!

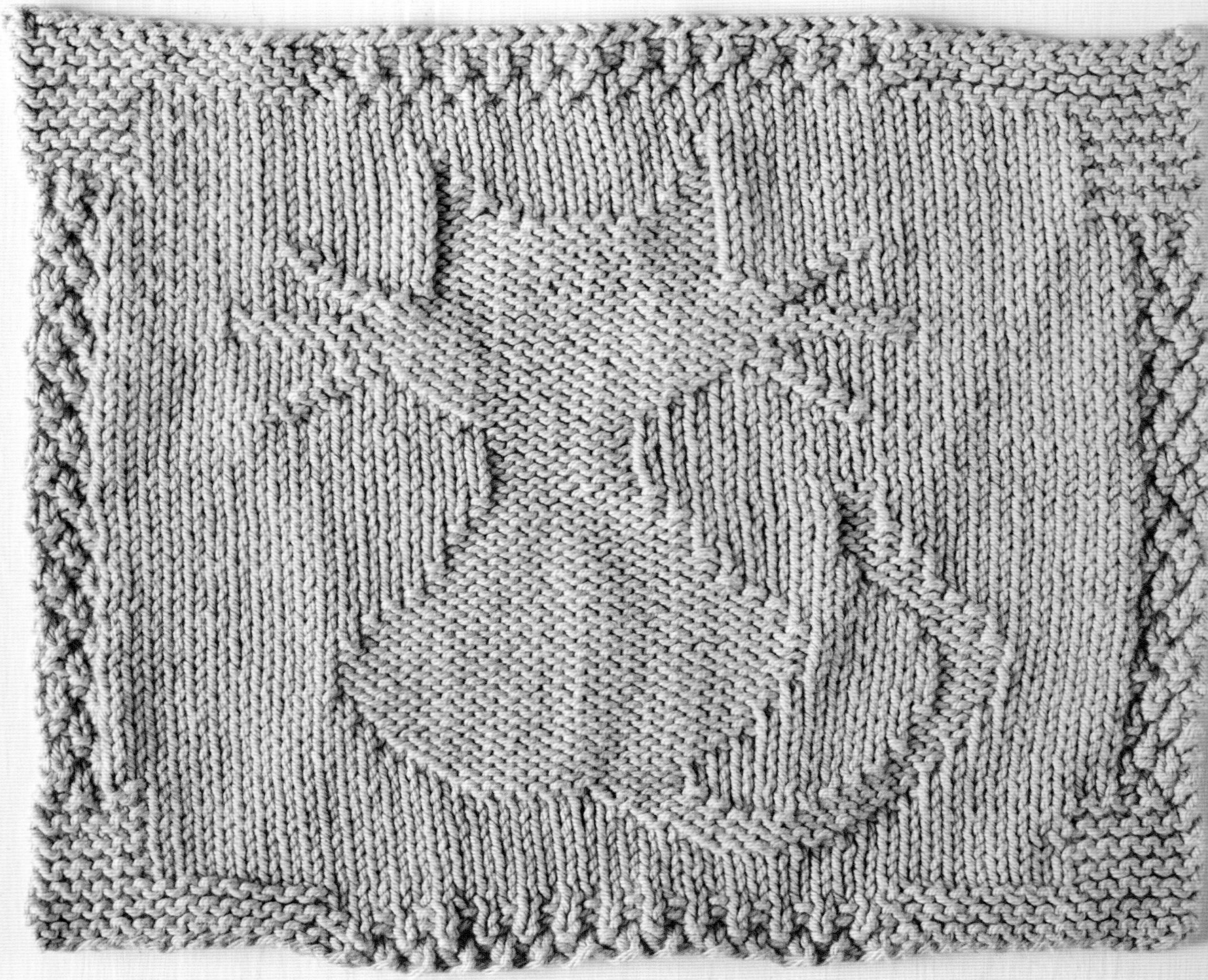

KITTEN KABOODLE DISHCLOTH

by Erica Jackofsky

What's new pussycat? This adorable dishcloth will have you singing while you're cleaning up the kitchen. A cute kitty is knit with a series of knits and purls surrounded by a garter and moss stitch border. Knit a few of these up and you'll be feline fine!

FINISHED MEASUREMENTS

Approximately 11" Square, blocked

YARN

Knit Picks Dishie (100% Cotton; 190 yards/100g): Linen 25400, 1 ball

NEEDLES

US 6 (4mm) straight or circular needles, or size to obtain gauge

GAUGE

20 sts and 25 rows = 4" in St st. (Gauge for this Project is approximate)

NOTIONS

Yarn Needle

Notes:

The Kitten Kaboodle pattern is provided in both written and chart form. If using the chart, read the charts RS rows (odd numbers) from right to left, and WS rows (even numbers) from left to right.

DIRECTIONS

CO 55 sts.

Work Rows 1-70 from written instructions or Kitten Kaboodle Dishcloth chart.

Row 1 (RS): K15, [P1, K1] 12 times, P1, K15.
Row 2 (WS): K14, [P1, K1] 13 times, P1, K14.
Row 3: K14, [P1, K1] 13 times, P1, K14.
Row 4: K15, [P1, K1] 12 times, P1, K15.
Row 5: K.
Row 6: K14, P27, K14.
Row 7: K.
Row 8: K6, P43, K6.
Row 9: K19, P4, K32.
Row 10: K6, P25, K7, P11, K6.
Row 11: K16, P10, K29.
Row 12: K6, P22, K5, P3, K4, P9, K6.
Row 13: K14, P4, K5, P5, K27.
Row 14: K6, P15, K10, P7, K4, P7, K6
Row 15: [K1, P1] twice, K9, P3, K8, P11, K16, [P1, K1] twice.
Row 16: [P1, K1] twice, P15, K13, P8, K3, P8, [K1, P1] twice.
Row 17: P1, K1, P1, K9, P3, K7, P15, K14, [K1, P1] twice.
Row 18: K1, P1, K1, P14, K17, P7, K3, P7, [P1, K1] twice.
Row 19: [K1, P1] twice, K7, P3, K7, P17, K13, [P1, K1] twice.
Row 20: [P1, K1] twice, P12, K19, P6, K3, P7, [K1, P1] twice.
Row 21: [P1, K1] twice, K6, P3, K7, P19, K12, [K1, P1] twice.
Row 22: [K1, P1] twice, P11, K21, P6, K3, P6, [P1, K1] twice.
Row 23: [K1, P1] twice, K6, P3, K6, P21, K11, [P1, K1] twice.
Row 24: [P1, K1] twice, P11, K21, P6, K3, P6, [K1, P1] twice.
Row 25: [P1, K1] twice, K6, P3, K6, P21, K11 [K1, P1] twice.
Row 26: [K1, P1] twice, P12, K19, P6, K3, P7, [P1, K1] twice.
Row 27: [K1, P1] twice, K7, P3, K6, P19, K12, [P1, K1] twice.
Row 28: [P1, K1] twice, P13, K17, P6, K3, P8, [K1, P1] twice.
Row 29: [P1, K1] twice, K9, P3, K6, P15, K14, [K1, P1] twice.
Row 30: [K1, P1] twice, P15, K13, P6, K3, P10, [P1, K1] twice.
Row 31: [K1, P1] twice, K10, P3, K6, P13, K15, [P1, K1] twice.
Row 32: [P1, K1] twice, P16, K11, P6, K3, P11, [K1, P1] twice.
Row 33: [P1, K1] twice, K11, P3, K6, P11, K16, [K1, P1] twice.
Row 34: [K1, P1] twice, P16, K11, P6, K2, P12, [P1, K1] twice.
Row 35: [K1, P1] twice, K12, P2, K7, P9, K17, [P1, K1] twice.
Row 36: [P1, K1] twice, P17, K9, P7, K2, P12, [K1, P1] twice.
Row 37: [P1, K1] twice, K22, P7, K18, [K1, P1] twice.
Row 38: [K1, P1] twice, P18, K7, P22, [P1, K1] twice.
Row 39: [K1, P1] twice, K22, P7, K18, [P1, K1] twice.
Row 40: [P1, K1] twice, P18, K7, P22, [K1, P1] twice.
Row 41: [P1, K1] twice, K22, P7, K18 [K1, P1] twice.
Row 42: [K1, P1] twice, P8, K2, P7, K9, P7, K2, P12, [P1, K1] twice.
Row 43: [K1, P1] twice, K13, P2, K5, P11, K5, P2, K9, [P1, K1] twice.
Row 44: [P1, K1] twice, P10, K2, P3, K13, P3, K2, P14, [K1, P1] twice.
Row 45: [P1, K1] twice, K15, P2, K1, P15, K1, P2, K11, [K1, P1] twice.
Row 46: [K1, P1] twice, P12, K19, P16, [P1, K1] twice.
Row 47: [K1, P1] twice, K17, P17, K13, [P1, K1] twice.
Row 48: [P1, K1] twice, P6, K31, P10, [K1, P1] twice.
Row 49: [P1, K1] twice, K10, P31, K6, [K1, P1] twice.
Row 50: [K1, P1] twice, P12, K19, P16, [P1, K1] twice.
Row 51: [K1, P1] twice, K15, P21, K11, [P1, K1] twice.
Row 52: [P1, K1] twice, P10, K2, P2, K15, P2, K2, P14, [K1, P1] twice.
Row 53: [P1, K1] twice, K13, P2, K4, P13, K4, P2, K9, [K1, P1] twice.
Row 54: [K1, P1] twice, P8, K2, P5, K13, P5, K2, P12, [P1, K1] twice.
Row 55: [K1, P1] twice, K19, P13, K15, [P1, K1] twice.
Row 56: [P1, K1] twice, P15, K13, P19, [K1, P1] twice.
Row 57: K23, P4, K5, P4, K19.
Row 58: K6, P13, K3, P7, K3, P17, K6.
Row 59: K23, P2, K9, P2, K19.
Row 60: K6, P13, K2, P9, K2, P17, K6.
Row 61: K23, P1, K11, P1, K19.
Row 62: K6, P13, K1, P11, K1, P17, K6.
Row 63: K.
Row 64: K6, P43, K6.
Row 65: K.
Row 66: K14, P27, K14.
Row 67: K14, [P1, K1] 13 times, P1, K14.
Row 68: K15, [P1, K1] 12 times, P1, K15.
Row 69: K15, [P1, K1] 12 times, P1, K15.
Row 70: K14, [P1, K1] 13 times, P1, K14.

BO all sts.

Finishing

Weave in ends, wash and block as necessary.

Kitten Kaboodle Chart

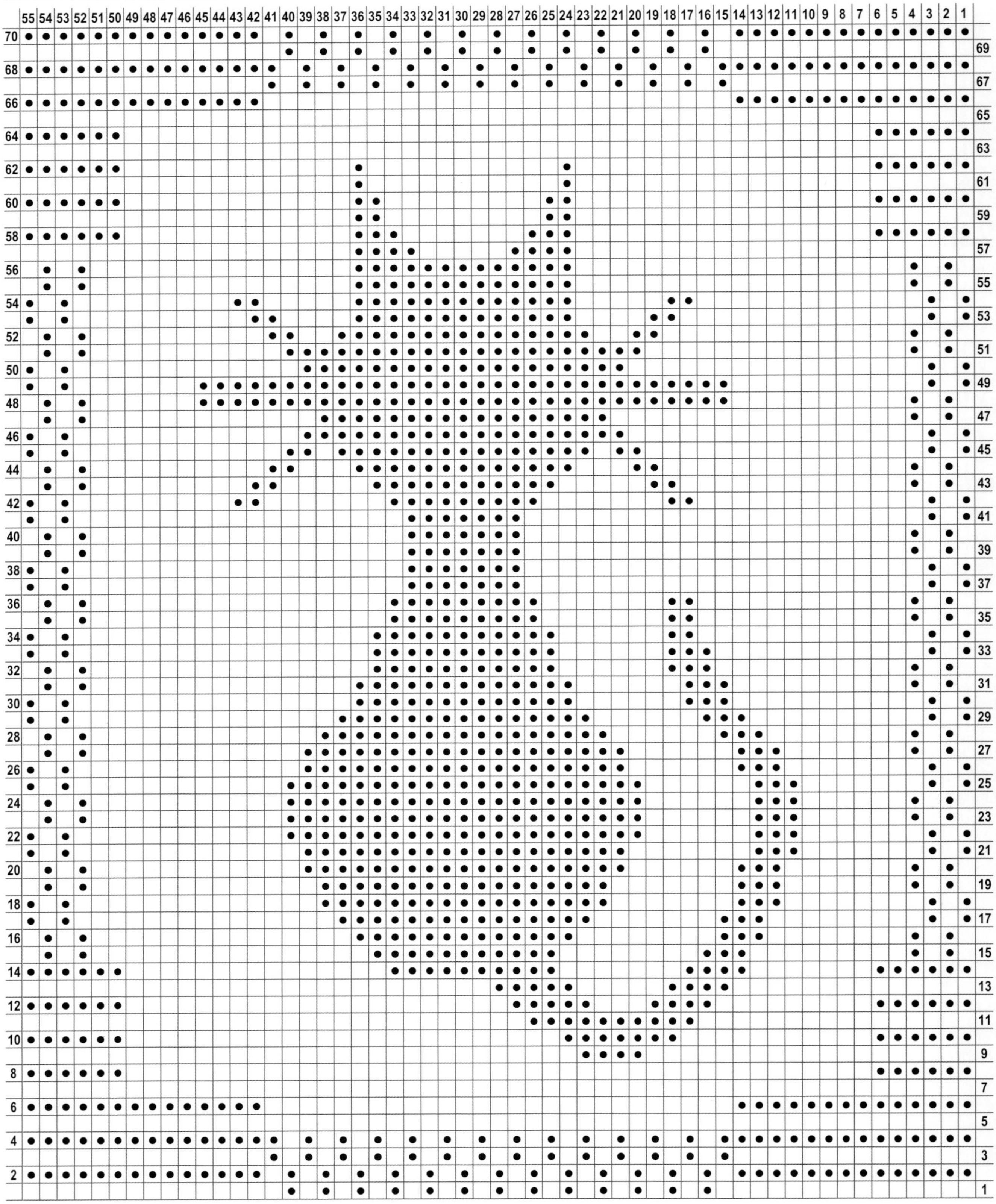

Legend

knit
☐ RS: knit stitch
WS: purl stitch

purl
⊡ RS: purl stitch
WS: knit stitch

EASY LACE DISHCLOTH

by Faith Schmidt

Easy Lace Dishcloth is a great introduction to lace knitting. Knitting this cloth in a lighter weight yarn would make a beautiful gift. Because of the open nature of the lace, this cloth is generously sized, but it can easily be resized to fit your needs.

FINISHED MEASUREMENTS

12.5" square, unblocked

YARN

Knit Picks Dishie (100% Cotton; 190 yards/100g): Kenai 25788, 1 ball

NEEDLES

US 5 (3.75mm) straight or circular needles, or size to obtain gauge

NOTIONS

Yarn Needle

GAUGE

15 sts and 26 rows = 4" over Easy Lace Stitch, unblocked
(Exact gauge is not important to this project.)

Notes:
To resize, CO a multiple of 5+2, and knit to desired length.

Easy Lace Stitch (worked flat over multiple of 5 sts plus 2)
Rows 1(RS): K1, *K2TOG, YO, K1, YO, SKP, repeat from * to last st, K1.
Rows 2 and 4 (WS): K1, P to last st, K1.
Row 3: K.
Repeat Rows 1-4 for pattern.

DIRECTIONS

CO 47 sts, using the Long Tail CO.
K 1 row.
Work Easy Lace St Rows 1-4 nineteen times total, then repeat Rows 1-2 once more.
BO P-wise on RS.

Finishing

Weave in ends. Block if desired.

HONEYCOMB DISHCLOTH

by Faith Schmidt

Honeycomb Dishcloth is a quick and fun knit. Increases and decreases paired with double yarn overs produce a lovely eyelet honeycomb pattern. It can easily be resized to fit your needs.

FINISHED MEASUREMENTS

Approximately 11 x 11.5", unblocked

YARN

Knit Picks Dishie (100% Cotton; 190 yards/100g): Mint 27041, 1 ball

NEEDLES

US 5 (3.75mm) straight or circular needles, or size to obtain gauge

NOTIONS

Yarn Needle

GAUGE

18 sts and 28 rows = 4" over Honeycomb Pattern, unblocked. Exact gauge is not important to this project

Notes:

On Rows 4 and 8, when you come to a double YO, knit into the first loop of the YO and purl into the second loop of the YO. Knit the rest of the row as directed by the pattern.

To resize, cast on a multiple of 4 plus 6 sts, and knit in pattern to desired length.

For assistance on the Long Tail CO, please see http://tutorials.knitpicks.com/long-tail-cast-on/

Honeycomb Pattern (worked flat over multiple of 4 plus 6 sts)

Row 1(RS): K.

Rows 2 and 6 (WS): K2, P to last 2 sts, K2.

Row 3: K3, *K2TOG, YO twice, SKP; rep from * to last 3 sts, K3.

Rows 4 and 8: K2, P to last 2 sts, K2. (See Note for Rows 4 and 8.)

Row 5: K.

Rows 7: K3, *YO, SKP, K2TOG, YO; repeat from * to last 3 sts, K3.

Rep Rows 1-8 for pattern.

DIRECTIONS

CO 50 sts, using the Long Tail CO method.

K 1 row.

Work Honeycomb Pattern (Rows 1-8) 9 times total. Then repeat Rows 1-5 once.

K 1 row.

BO all sts K-wise.

Finishing

Weave in ends. Block if desired.

NEELI FACECLOTH

by Joyce Fassbender

A soft and gentle facecloth is wonderful after a long day. Knit in Comfy Fingering with a textured pattern surround by moss stitch, the Neeli Facecloth is a beautiful as it is useful. Relax with your own handmade facecloth or gift as part of a set.

FINISHED MEASUREMENTS

7.25" wide x 7.5" high

YARN

Knit Picks Comfy Fingering (75% Pima Cotton, 25% Acrylic; 218 yards/50g): Peapod 24830, 1 ball

NEEDLES

US 2 (2.75) straight or circular needles, or size to obtain gauge

NOTIONS

Yarn Needle

GAUGE

29 sts and 36 rows = 4" in Chart pattern, blocked

Notes: The cloth is charted with a textured center surrounded by a moss stitch edge. Boxed stitch pattern repeat is worked two times across each row. Read the charts RS rows (odd numbers) from right to left, and WS rows (even numbers) from left to right.

DIRECTIONS

CO 53 sts using the Long Tail CO.

Set Up Rows

Rows 1 and 2: (K1, P1) to last stitch, K1.

Rows 3 and 4: (P1, K1) to last stitch, P1.

Work Chart

Work Rows 1-20 of Chart 1 three times. The boxed stitch pattern repeat is worked two times per row.

End Rows

Rows 1 and 2: (K1, P1) to last st, K1.

Rows 3 and 4: (P1, K1) to last st, P1.

Finishing

BO all sts. Weave in ends, wash and block.

Neeli Chart

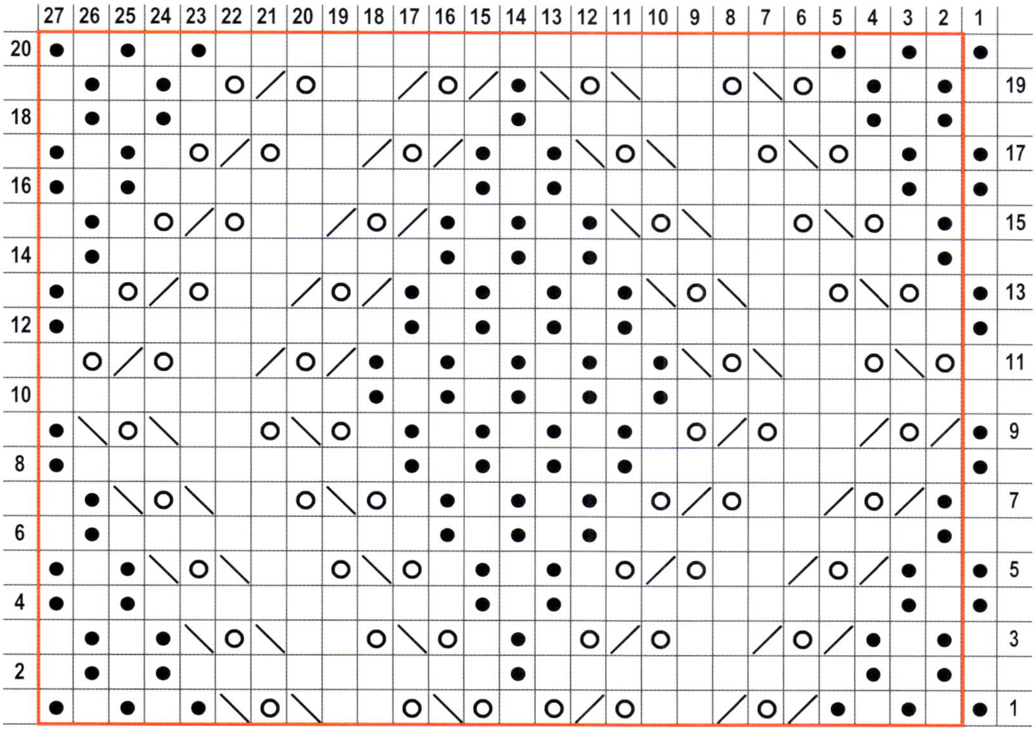

Legend:

- **purl** — RS: purl stitch; WS: knit stitch
- **knit** — RS: knit stitch; WS: purl stitch
- **k2tog** — Knit two stitch
- **yo** — Yarn Over
- **ssk** — Slip one stitch as if to knit, Slip another stitch as if to knit. Insert left-hand needle into front of these 2 stitches and knit them together

NEOSCONA FACECLOTH

by Joyce Fassbender

Inspired by beautiful spiderwebs, this facecloth is perfect for practicing your lace skills. Knit in the round from the inside out, this design features increases, decreases and nupps on a fully charted design. Choose your favorite spooky color for a true spiderweb or go lighter for an elegant piece

FINISHED MEASUREMENTS

11.75" diameter, blocked

YARN

Knit Picks Shine Sport (60% Pima Cotton, 40% Modal; 110 yards/50g): Grapefruit 25778, 1 ball

NEEDLES

US 4 (3.5mm) DPNs and 16" circular needles, or size to obtain gauge

NOTIONS

Yarn Needle

GAUGE

22 sts and 30 rows = 4" in St st in the rnd, blocked

Notes:

This washcloth is worked in the round from the center outward. The stitch pattern is fully charted.

Circular Cast On

Pinch the working yarn between the first and middle finger of your left hand so the end of the yarn comes out behind your fingers. Wrap the working yarn tail around the ring and pinky fingers of your left hand, holding the yarn tail firmly with your right hand. Point the tips of these fingers down toward your palm. *Using your right hand, insert the point of your needle (you can use DPNs or a circular needle) under the yarn across the back of your ring and pinky fingers (the 'first loop') from front to back, pass the needle over the working yarn and draw a loop out from under the first loop (this creates one CO st), YO.* Repeat from * to * until you have CO the required number of sts. Note: If you need an even number of sts, you will need to CO the final st as a standard YO when you begin your first rnd of knitting. Arrange the sts on your DPNs to begin knitting in the rnd.
Tug on the yarn tail to draw the sts into a tighter circle.

Nupp 5: In one st, KFB two times, K1. (Results in five sts in one st.) Turn work, P these five sts. Turn work, K the five sts. Turn work, P the five sts. Turn work, starting with last st and working one st at a time, pass 4 sts over first st.

Nupp 7: In one st, KFB three times, K1. (Results in seven sts in one st.) Turn work, P these seven sts. Turn work, K the seven sts. Turn work, P the seven sts. Turn work, starting with last st and working one st at a time, pass 6 sts over first st.

DIRECTIONS

CO 8 sts using a Circular CO. PM and join in the rnd, taking care not to twist sts.

Set Up Rows

Rnd 1: K.

Rnd 2: (YO, K1) eight times. 16 sts.

Rnd 3: K.

Work Chart

Work Rnds 1-40 of Chart 8 times around. All chart rnds are read from right to left as RS rows. Switch from DPNs to circular needles as needed.

Finishing

BO loosely. Weave in ends, wash and block.

Neoscona Chart

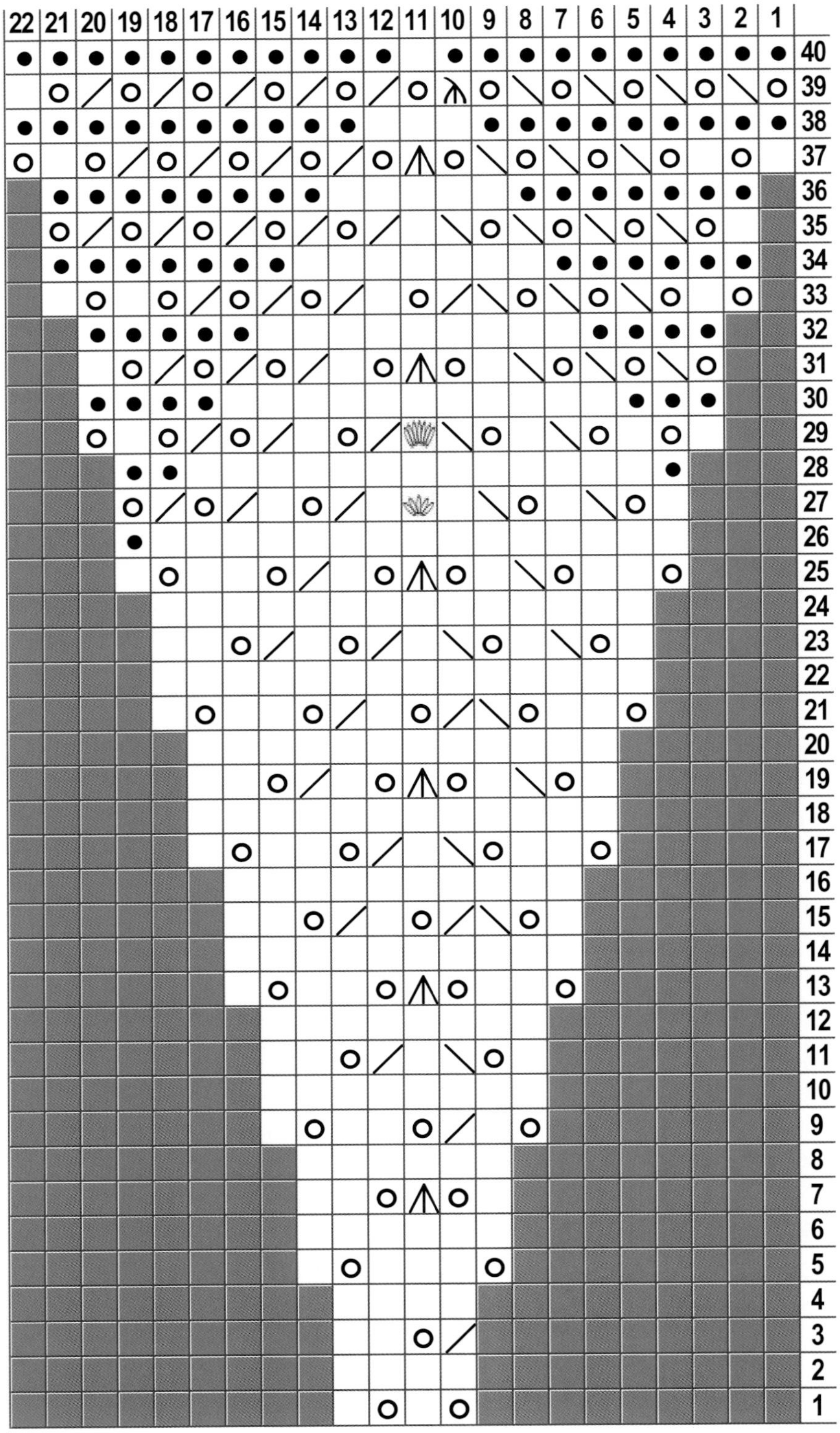

Legend

No Stitch
Placeholder - No stitch made.

yo
Yarn Over

knit
Knit stitch

purl
Purl stitch

k2tog
Knit two stitches together as one stitch

Central Double Dec
Slip first and second stitches together as if to knit. Knit 1 stitch. Pass two slipped stitches over the knit stitch.

ssk
Slip one stitch as if to knit, Slip another stitch as if to knit. Insert left-hand needle into front of these 2 stitches and knit them together

sl1 k2tog psso
Slip 1, k2tog, pass slip stitch over k2tog

nupp5
In one st, KFB two times, K1. (Results in five sts in one st.) Turn work, P these five sts. Turn work, K the five sts. Turn work, P the five sts. Turn work, starting with last st and working one st at a time, pass 4 sts over first st.

nupp7
In one st, KFB three times, K1. (Results in seven sts in one st.) Turn work, P these seven sts. Turn work, K the seven sts. Turn work, P the seven sts. Turn work, starting with last st and working one st at a time, pass 6 sts over first st.

RIPPLING DIAMONDS FACECLOTH

by Allison Griffith

Explore the fun of texture with this quick and fun project! This washcloth is knit from the bottom up in a single piece. A garter stitch border is worked around the edge of a charted pattern of knits and purls.

FINISHED MEASUREMENTS

7" wide x 8.75" high

YARN

Knit Picks Dishie (100% Cotton; 190 yards/100g): Azure 25412, 1 ball

NEEDLES

US 8 (4.5mm) straight or circular needles, or size to obtain gauge

NOTIONS

Yarn Needle

GAUGE

21 sts and 28 rows = 4" over texture pattern, blocked

Notes:

Read the charts RS rows (odd numbers) from right to left, and WS rows (even numbers) from left to right.

DIRECTIONS

CO 37 sts and prepare to work back and forth.

K 6 rows.

Work Rippling Diamonds Chart, Rows 1-50.

K 6 rows.

BO loosely.

Finishing

Weave in ends, and block lightly.

Rippling Diamonds Chart

Legend

- ☐ **knit** RS: knit stitch WS: purl stitch
- ⊡ **purl** RS: purl stitch WS: knit stitch

PRESENT DISHCLOTH

by Allyson Dykhuizen

Who doesn't enjoy getting a little present out of the blue? This dishcloth will give you practice with some light intarsia and the whole project is wrapped up with an icord bow. Perfect as an extra decoration for any gift!

FINISHED MEASUREMENTS

6.25" wide x 7" tall, blocked

YARN

Knit Picks CotLin (70% Tanguis Cotton, 30% Linen; 123 yards/50g): C1 Eggplant 26998, C2 Whisper 25328, 1 ball each

NEEDLES

US 5 (3.75mm) DPNs and straight or circular needles, or size to obtain gauge

NOTIONS

Yarn Needle

GAUGE

22 sts and 36 Rows = 4" in Garter stitch, blocked

Notes:

This dishcloth is worked from the bottom up. To create a center stripe you'll need to create 2 balls of C1 by splitting the ball into 2 even balls before getting started.

I-Cord

Using DPNs, CO 3 sts. K 1 Row. Do not turn.

Row 1: Sl sts to other end of the needle they are on. K3, do not turn.

Rep Row 1 until I-Cord is desired length.

Cut yarn and thread tail through all sts. Pull tight.

DIRECTIONS

With C1, CO 35 sts.

Row 1 (RS): With C1, Sl1, K13; with C2, K7; with second ball of C1, K14.

Row 2 (WS): With C1, Sl1, K13; with C2, P7; with second ball of C1, K14.

Rep these 2 rows until piece measures 3". Cut all strands.

Row 1 (RS): With C2, Sl1; K to end.

Row 2 (WS): With C2, Sl1, P to end.

Rep these 2 rows 3 times more.

Row 1 (RS): With C1, Sl1, K13; with C2, K7, with second ball of C1, K14.

Row 2 (WS): With C1 Sl1, K13; with C2, P7, with second ball of C1, K14.

Rep these 2 rows until piece measures 7". With first ball of C1, BO first 14 sts; with C2, BO center 7 sts; with second ball of C1, BO last 14 sts.

Bow

With C2 and DPNs, CO 3 sts. Make a 18" I-Cord. Weave in ends. Tie the I-Cord in half loosely. Make a bow with about 6" loops, and ends between 1.5-3.5" long. It's cute to make them different lengths!

Finishing

Weave in ends. Seam center of bow to top of dishcloth. Wash and block to measurements.

SNOWFLAKE DISHCLOTH

by Allyson Dykhuizen

Celebrate the winter season with this pretty snowflake dishcloth! The unique shape is constructed by working the piece from the center out. Stitches are held as different sections of the snowflake are worked and holes are created with casting on additional stitches. For a finishing touch, points are made with mirrored decreases. You'll have your own special snowflake in no time at all.

FINISHED MEASUREMENTS
8.5" across

YARN
Knit Picks CotLin (70% Tanguis Cotton, 30% Linen; 123 yards/50g): Clarity 26997, 1 ball

NEEDLES
US 5 (3.75mm) DPNs and 16" circular needle, or size to obtain gauge

NOTIONS
Stitch Marker
Yarn Needle

GAUGE
22 sts and 36 rnds = 4" in garter stitch, blocked

DIRECTIONS

Center

CO 6 sts. Divide sts evenly between 3 DPNs, 2 sts each needle. PM and join to work in the round.

Rnd 1 and all odd rnds through Rnd 9: Purl.
Rnd 2: KFB around - 12 sts.
Rnd 4: [K1, KFB] around - 18 sts.
Rnd 6: [K2, KFB] around - 24 sts.
Rnd 8: [K3, KFB] around - 30 sts.
Rnd 9: Purl.

Inner Ice Crystal

Row 10 (RS): K10, turn. Leave unworked sts on needles or move them to scrap yarn.
Rows 11-13: K10.
CO 4 sts - 14 sts.
Cut yarn. Return next 10 sts to needles and with RS facing, reattach yarn to work Inner Ice Crystal again. Rep again over last 10 sts - 3 Inner Ice Crystals worked and 42 total stitches on needles.

Rnd 14 (RS): [K6, KFB] around, joining all Ice Crystals to work in the rnd - 48 sts.
Rnds 15, 17, and 19: Purl.
Rnd 16: [K7, KFB] around - 54 sts.
Rnd 18: [K8, KFB] around - 60 sts.

Middle Ice Crystal

Row 20 (RS): K10, turn. Leave unworked sts on needles or move them to scrap yarn.
Rows 21-23: Knit. CO 2 sts - 12 sts. Place these sts on circular needle.
Cut yarn. Return next 10 sts to needles and with RS facing, reattach yarn to work Middle Ice Crystal again. Rep to make 6 Middle Ice Crystals total - 6 Middle Ice Crystals worked and 72 total stitches on circular needle.
Rnd 24: [K11, KFB] around - 78 sts.
Rnd 25, 27, and 29: Purl.
Rnd 26: [K12, KFB] around - 84 sts.
Rnd 28: [K13, KFB] around - 90 sts.
Rnd 29: Purl.

Outer Ice Crystal

Row 30 (RS): K10, turn. Leave unworked sts on needles or move them to scrap yarn.
Row 31 (WS): K1, P1, K6, P1, K1.
Row 32: Knit.
Row 33: K1, P1, K6, P1, K1.
Row 34: K1, SSK, K4, K2tog, K1 - 8 sts.
Row 35: K1, P1, K4, P1, K1.
Row 36: K1, SSK, K2, K2tog, K1 - 6 sts.
Row 37: K1, P1, K2, P1, K1.
Row 38: K1, SSK, K2tog, K1 - 4 sts.
BO sts.
Cut yarn. Return next 10 sts to needles and with RS facing, reattach yarn to work Outer Ice Crystal again over next 10 sts. Rep to make 9 Outer Ice Crystals around work.

Finishing

Weave in ends, wash and block to measurements.

FESTIVE WREATH DISHCLOTH

by Ann Weaver

FINISHED MEASUREMENTS

11" diameter, blocked

YARN

Knit Picks Dishie (100% Cotton; 190 yards/100g): C1 Jalapeno 25785, C2 Fiesta Red 25786; 1 ball each

NEEDLES

US 7 (4.5mm) DPNs, 16" and 24" circular needles, or size to obtain gauge

NOTIONS

Yarn Needle
Stitch Marker

GAUGE

20 sts and 24 rnds = 4" in St st in the rnd, blocked

Notes:
This dishcloth uses the Circular Cast On. You can find a tutorial for the
Circular Cast On here: http://tutorials.knitpicks.com/wptutorials/circular-cast-on/.

DIRECTIONS

Using the Circular CO and DPNs, with C1, CO 9 sts. Arrange the sts on three DPNs so there are 3 sts on each DPN. PM to indicate the beginning of the rnd.
K 1 rnd.
Inc Rnd: KFB to end. 18 sts.

Section 1

Rnd 1: With C1, K.
Rnd 2: With C2, K.
Inc Rnd: With C1, KFB to end. 36 sts.

Section 2

Rnd 1: With C2, K.
Rnd 2: With C1, K.
Rep Rnds 1-2 once more, then rep Rnd 1 once more. 5 rnds total.
Cut C2.
Inc Rnd: With C1, KFB to end. 72 sts.
At this point, you likely will be able to transfer your sts from the DPNs to the 16" circular needle.

Section 3

Rnd 1: (K4, YO, K1, YO, K4, SK2P) 6 times.
Rnd 2: Remove M, K1, PM, [(K3, YO) twice, K3, SK2P] 6 times.
Rnd 3: Remove M, K1, PM, (K2, YO, K5, YO, K2, SK2P) 6 times.
Rnd 4: Remove M, K1, PM, (K1, YO, K7, YO, K1, SK2P) 6 times.
Rnd 5: Remove M, K1, PM, (YO, K9, YO, SK2P) 6 times.
Rnd 6: (YO, K4, SK2P, K4, YO, K1) 6 times.
Rnd 7: K1, YO, [K3, SK2P, (K3, YO) twice] 5 times, K3, SK2P, K3, YO, K2.
Rnd 8: K2, YO, K2, (SK2P, K2, YO, K5, YO, K2) 5 times, SK2P, K2, YO, K3.
Rnd 9: K3, (YO, K1, SK2P, K1, YO, K7) 5 times, YO, K1, SK2P, K1, YO, K4.
Rnd 10: K4, (YO, SK2P, YO, K9) 5 times, YO, SK2P, YO, K5.
Rnd 11: K.
Inc Rnd: (K1, YO) to end. 144 sts.
At this point, you likely will be able to transfer your sts from the 16" circular needle to the 24" circular needle.

Section 4

Join C2.
Rnd 1: With C2, [(K1, YO) twice, K2tog twice, (K1, YO) twice] 18 times.
Rnd 2: With C2, P.
Rnds 3 and 4: With C1, K.
Rep Rnds 1-4 once more, then rep Rnds 1-2 once more. 9 rnds total.
BO using two-color BO as follows: *With C1, K1; with C2, K1; pass first st over second st; rep from * until all sts are bound off.
Pull yarn through last st and pull tight.

Finishing

Weave in ends, block and enjoy!

TRIANGLE SQUARED DISHCLOTH

by Erica Jackofsky

FINISHED MEASUREMENTS

Approximately 11" Rounded Square, blocked

YARN

Knit Picks CotLin (70% Tanguis Cotton, 30% Linen; 123 yards/50g): Sagebrush 25777, 1 ball

NEEDLES

US 3 (3.25mm) DPNs and 16" circular needles, or size to obtain gauge

NOTIONS

Yarn Needle

GAUGE

24 sts and 42 rnds = 4" in St st in the rnd, blocked. (Gauge for this project is approximate)

Notes:

Although this dishcloth lays flat when finished, you will be working in the round.

Triangle Squared Pattern (worked in the rnd)

Rnd 1: (K1, P1, K1) 4 times.

Rnd 2: (K1, YO, P1, YO, K1) 4 times. 20 sts.

Rnd 3: (K1, P1 TBL, P1, P1 TBL, K1) 4 times.

Rnd 4: (K1, YO, P3, YO, K1) 4 times. 28 sts.

Rnd 5: (K1, K1 TBL, P3, K1 TBL, K1) 4 times.

Rnd 6: (K1, YO, K1, P3, K1, YO, K1) 4 times. 36 sts.

Rnd 7: (K1, K1 TBL, K1, P3, K1, K1 TBL, K1) 4 times.

Rnd 8: (K1, YO, K2, P3, K2, YO, K1) 4 times. 44 sts

Rnd 9: (K1, K1 TBL, K2, P3, K2, K1 TBL, K1) 4 times.

Rnd 10: (K1, YO, K3, P3, K3, YO, K1) 4 times. 52 sts.

Rnd 11: (K1, K1 TBL, K3, P3, K3, K1 TBL, K1) 4 times.

Rnd 12: (K1, YO, K4, P3, K4, YO, K1) 4 times. 60 sts.

Rnd 13: (K1, K1 TBL, K4, P3, K4, K1 TBL, K1) 4 times.

Rnd 14: (K1, YO, P1, K4, P3, K4, P1, YO, K1) 4 times. 68 sts.

Rnd 15: (K1, K1 TBL, P2, K3, P3, K3, P2, K1 TBL, K1) 4 times.

Rnd 16: (K1, YO, K1, (P3, K2) twice, P3, K1, YO, K1) 4 times. 76 sts.

Rnd 17: (K1, K1 TBL, K1, P4, K1, P3, K1, P4, K1, K1 TBL, K1) 4 times.

Rnd 18: (K1, YO, K2, P13, K2, YO, K1) 4 times. 84 sts.

Rnd 19: (K1, K1 TBL, K2, P4, K1, P3, K1, P4, K2, K1 TBL, K1) 4 times.

Rnd 20: (K1, YO, K3, P3, (K2, P3) twice, K3, YO, K1) 4 times. 92 sts.

Rnd 21: (K1, K1 TBL, K3, P2, K3, P3, K3, P2, K3, K1 TBL, K1) 4 times.

Rnd 22: (K1, YO, K4, P1, K4, P3, K4, P1, K4, YO, K1) 4 times. 100 sts.

Rnd 23: (K1, K1 TBL, K9, P3, K9, K1 TBL, K1) 4 times.

Rnd 24: (K1, YO, K2, P1, K2, P1, K4, P3, K4, P1, K2, P1, K2, YO, K1) 4 times. 108 sts.

Rnd 25: (K1, K1 TBL, K1, P2, K2, P2, K3, P3, K3, P2, K2, P2, K1, K1 TBL, K1) 4 times.

Rnd 26: (K1, YO, K1, (P3, K2) 4 times, P3, K1, YO, K1) 4 times.116 sts.

Rnd 27: (K1, K1 TBL, P4, K2, P4, K1, P3, K1, P4, K2, P4, K1 TBL, K1) 4 times.

Rnd 28: (K1, YO, P5, K2, P13, K2, P5, YO, K1) 4 times. 124 sts.

Rnd 29: (K1, P1 TBL, K1, P4, K2, P4, K1, P3, K1, P4, K2, P4, K1, P1 TBL, K1) 4 times.

Rnd 30: (K1, YO, P1, (K2, P3) 5 times, K2, P1, YO, K1) 4 times.132 sts.

Rnd 31: (K1, P1 TBL, P1, K3, P2, K2, P2, K3, P3, K3, P2, K2, P2, K3, P1, P1 TBL, K1) 4 times.

Rnd 32: (K1, YO, P2, K4, P1, K2, P1, K4, P3, K4, P1, K2, P1, K4, P2, YO, K1) 4 times. 140 sts.

Rnd 33: (K1, K1 TBL, P2, K12, P3, K12, P2, K1 TBL, K1) 4 times.

Rnd 34: (K1, YO, K1, P2, K4, P1, K2, P1, K4, P3, K4, P1, K2, P1, K4, P2, K1, YO, K1) 4 times. 148 sts.

Rnd 35: (K1, K1 TBL, K1, P2, K3, P2, K2, P2, K3, P3, K3, P2, K2, P2, K3, P2, K1, K1 TBL, K1) 4 times.

Rnd 36: (K1, YO, K2, P2, K2, (P3, K2) 5 times, P2, K2, YO, K1) 4 times. 156 sts.

Rnd 37: (K1, K1 TBL, K2, P2, K1, P4, K2, P4, K1, P3, K1, P4, K2, P4, K1, P2, K2, K1TBL, K1) 4 times.

Rnd 38: (K1, YO, K3, P7, K2, P13, K2, P7, K3, YO, K1) 4 times. 164 sts.

Rnd 39: (K1, K1 TBL, K3, P2, K1, P4, K2, P4, K1, P3, K1, P4, K2, P4, K1, P2, K3, K1TBL, K1) 4 times.

Rnd 40: (K1, YO, K4, P2, (K2, P3) 5 times, K2, P2, K4, YO, K1) 4 times. 172 sts.

Rnd 41: (K1, K1 TBL, K4, P2, K3, P2, K2, P2, K3, P3, K3, P2, K2, P2, K3, P2, K4, K1TBL, K1) 4 times.

Rnd 42: (K1, YO, K5, P2, K4, P1, K2, P1, K4, P3, K4, P1, K2, P1, K4, P2, K5, YO, K1) 4 times. 180 sts.

Rnd 43: (K1, K1 TBL, K5, P2, K12, P3, K12, P2, K5, K1 TBL, K1) 4 times.

Rnd 44: (K1, YO, K1, P1, K4, P2, K4, P1, K2, P1, K4, P3, K4, P1, K2, P1, K4, P2, K4, P1, K1, YO, K1) 4 times. 188 sts.

Rnd 45: (K1, K1 TBL, K1, (P2, K3) twice, P2, K2, P2, K3, P3, K3, P2, K2, (P2, K3) twice, P2, K1, K1 TBL, K1) 4 times.

Rnd 46: (K1, YO, K2, P3, K2, P2, (K2, P3) 5 times, K2, P2, K2, P3, K2, YO, K1) 4 times. 196 sts.

Rnd 47: (K1, K1 TBL, K2, P4, K1, P2, K1, P4, K2, P4, K1, P3, K1, P4, K2, P4, K1, P2, K1, P4, K2, K1 TBL, K1) 4 times.

Rnd 48: (K1, YO, K3, P12, K2, P13, K2, P12, K3, YO, K1) 4 times. 204 sts.

Rnd 49: (K1, K1 TBL, K3, P4, K1, P2, K1, P4, K2, P4, K1, P3, K1, P4, K2, P4, K1, P2, K1, P4, K3, K1TBL, K1) 4 times.

Rnd 50: (K1, YO, K4, P3, K2, P2, (K2, P3) 5 times, K2, P2, K2, P3, K4, YO, K1) 4 times. 212 sts.

Rnd 51: (K1, K1 TBL, K4, (P2, K3) twice, P2, K2, P2, K3, P3, K3, P2, K2, (P2, K3) twice, P2, K4, K1 TBL, K1) 4 times.

Rnd 52: (K1, YO, K5, P1, K4, P2, K4, P1, K2, P1, K4, P3, K4, P1, K2, P1, K4, P2, K4, P1, K5, YO, K1) 4 times. 220 sts.

Rnd 53: (K1, K1 TBL, K10, P2, K12, P3, K12, P2, K10, K1 TBL, K1, YO) 4 times. 224 sts.

When working from the Chart in the rnd, follow all Chart rows from right to left, reading them as RS rows.

DIRECTIONS

With DPNs, CO 4 sts.

Rnd 1: KFB 4 times. 8 sts.

Rnd 2: (K1, YO, K1) 4 times. 12 sts.

Work Rnds 1-53 of Triangle Squared Pattern from Chart (worked 4 times around) or written instructions. Switch to circular needles when there are too many sts to comfortably work on DPNs.

Finishing

Applied I-cord BO

CO 2 sts on left needle, K3, slide these sts back to left hand needle, *K2, Sl1, K1, PSSO. 3 sts on right needle. Sl these sts back to left hand needle; rep from * until all picked up sts are worked. 3 sts remain. Fasten off and sew the end down.

Weave in ends, wash and block as necessary.

Triangle Squared Chart

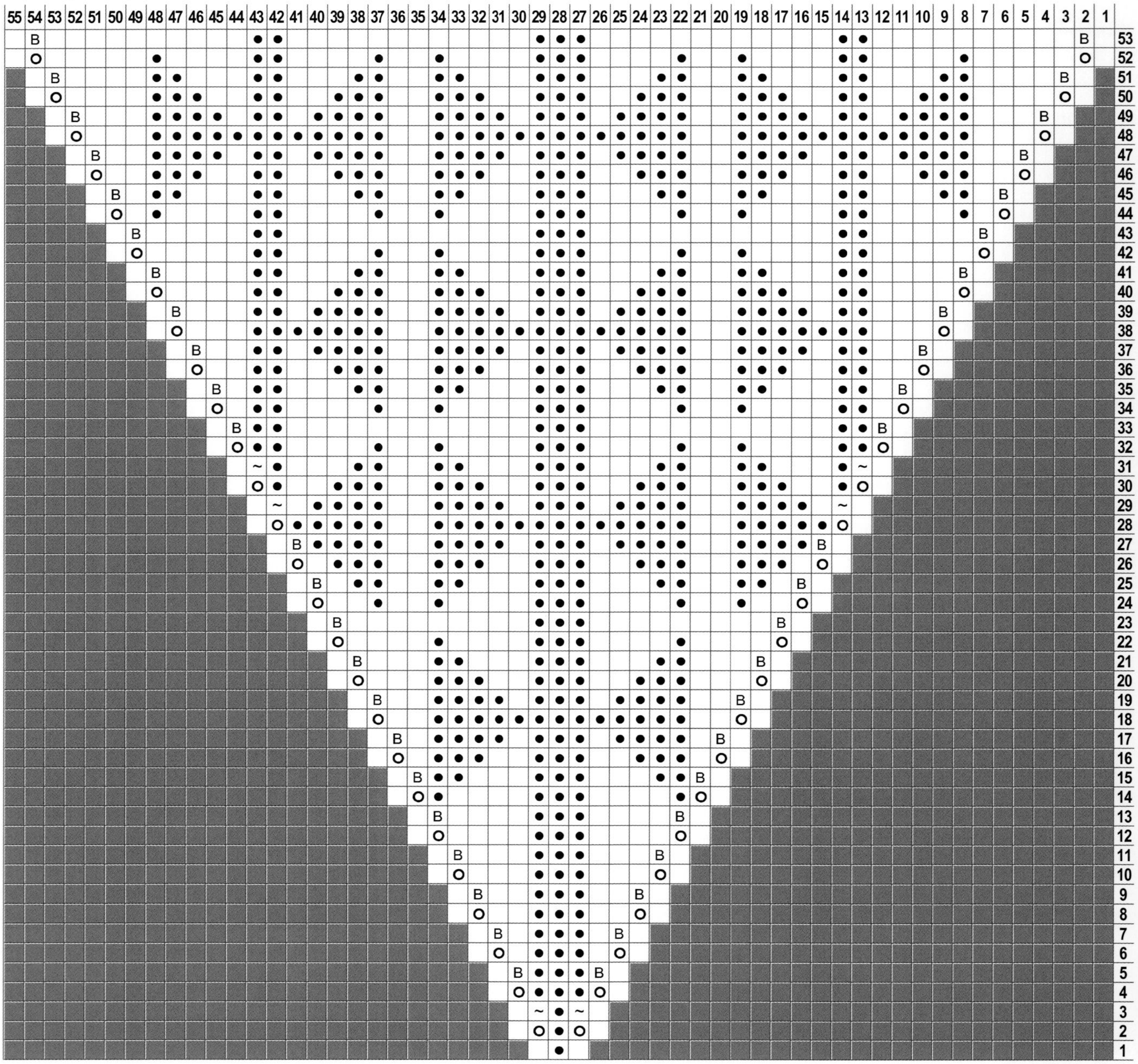

Legend

- **No Stitch** Placeholder - No stitch made.
- **knit** knit stitch
- **purl** purl stitch
- **yo** Yarn Over
- **purl tbl** Purl stitch through the back loop
- **knit tbl** Knit stitch through back loop

Liriactis Chart

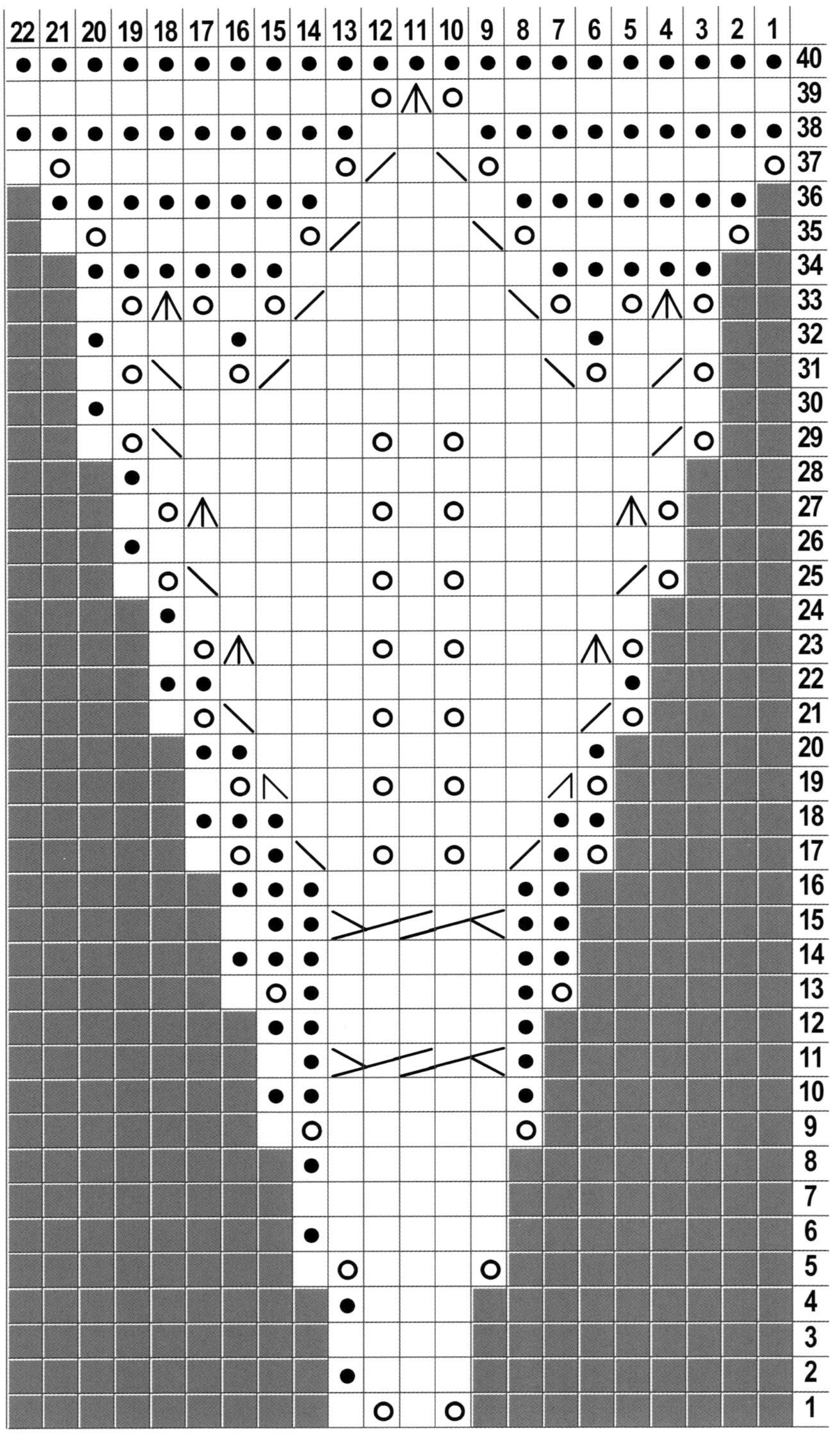

Legend

No Stitch
Placeholder - No stitch made.

yo
Yarn Over

knit
knit stitch

purl
purl stitch

2/3RC
sl3 to CN, hold in back. k2, then k3 from CN

k2tog
Knit two stitches together as one stitch

ssk
Slip one stitch as if to knit, Slip another stitch as if to knit. Insert left-hand needle into front of these 2 stitches and knit them together

k3 tog
Knit three stitches together as one

k3tog tbl
Knit three stitches together through back loops

Central Double Dec
Slip first and second stitches together as if to knit. Knit 1 stitch. Pass two slipped stitches over the knit stitch.

Desert Arrow Chart

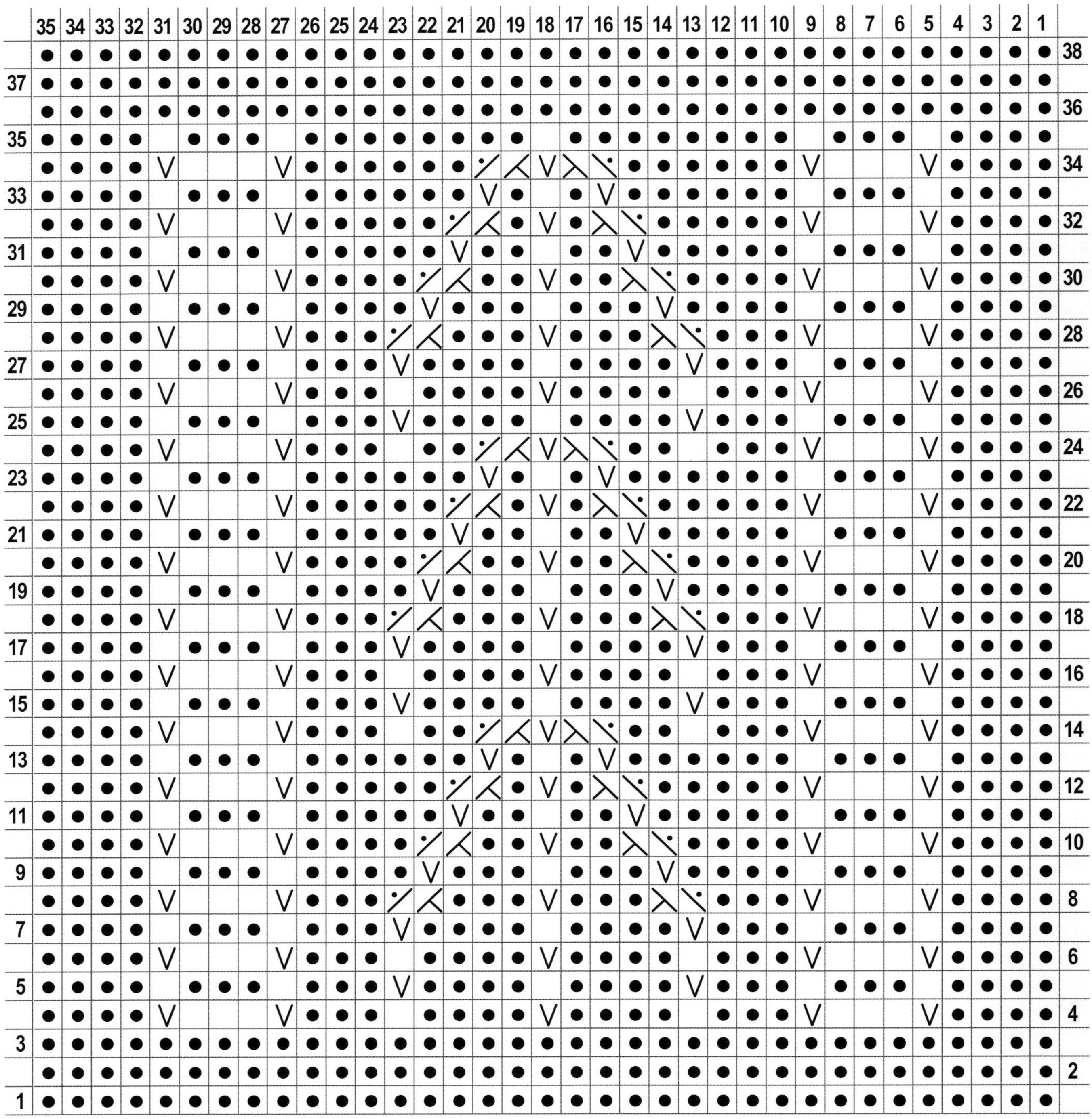

Legend

purl
RS: purl stitch
WS: knit stitch

slip
RS: Slip stitch as if to purl, holding yarn in back
WS: Slip stitch as if to purl, holding yarn in front

knit
RS: knit stitch
WS: purl stitch

1/1 LPC
WYIF, P into back loop of second st on left-hand needle; WYIB, K in front loop of first st on left-hand needle, drop both sts off of left-hand needle.

1/1 RPC
Skip first st on left-hand needle WYIB, K through front loop of second st on left-hand needle, pull the st through to the front of work; WYIF, P front loop of first st, drop both sts off of left-hand needle

CERAMIC DISHCLOTH

by Kalurah Hudson

A unique slip stitch pattern creates the traveling and twisting cables in this striking dishcloth. The raised relief design resembles pretty, slip-embossed ceramic pottery. The 2 stitch I-cord bind off adds a polished finish, with a handy corner loop for hanging from a cabinet knob or hook.

FINISHED MEASUREMENTS

11" high x 12" wide, blocked

YARN

Knit Picks Shine Worsted (60% Pima Cotton, 40% Modal; 75 yards/50g): Cream 23799, 2 balls

NEEDLES

US 8 (5mm) straight or 24" circular needles, or size to obtain gauge

NOTIONS

Yarn Needle

GAUGE

16 sts and 20 rows = 4" in Reverse St st, blocked

Notes:

Sl WYIF

Slip st P-wise with yarn held in front.

1/1 LC

Knit into back of second stitch on LH (from right to left), knit into front loop of first stitch on LH needle, drop both sts off of LH needle.

1/1 LPC

WYIF, purl into back loop of second stitch on LH needle, bring yarn to front of work, knit in front loop of first stitch on LH needle, drop both sts off of LH needle.

1/1 RPC

Skip first stitch on LH needle. WYIB, knit through front loop of second stitch on LH needle, pull the stitch through to the front of work, bring yarn to front of work, purl front loop of first stitch, drop both sts off of LH needle.

Written Instructions (worked flat over 48 sts)

Row 1 (WS): Knit
Row 2 (RS): Purl
Row 3: Knit
Row 4: Purl
Row 5: K5, sl wyif x 2, K2, [sl wyif, K4, sl wyif x 2, K2, sl wyif, K2] 3x, K3.
Row 6: P3, [P2, 1/1 LC, P2, K1, P4, K1] 3x, P2, 1/1 LC, P5.
Row 7: Repeat row 5.
Row 8: P3, [P1, 1/1 RPC, 1/1 LPC, P1, K1, P4, K1)] 3x, P1, 1/1 RPC, 1/1 LPC, P4.
Row 9: K4, sl wyif, K2, sl wyif, K1, [sl wyif, K4, sl wyif, K1, sl wyif, K2, sl wyif, K1] 3x, K3.
Row 10: P3, [1/1 RPC, P2, 1/1 LPC x2, P2, 1/1 RPC] 3x, 1/1 RPC, P2, 1/1 LPC, P3
Row 11: K3, sl wyif, K4, sl wyif, [K1, sl wyif, K2, sl wyif, K1, sl wyif, K4, sl wyif] 3x, K3.
Row 12: P3, [K1, P4, K1, P1, 1/1 LPC, 1/1 RPC, P1] 3x, K1, P4, K1, P3.
Row 13: K3, sl wyif, K4, sl wyif, [K2, sl wyif x 2, K2, sl wyif, K4, sl wyif] 3x, K3.
Row 14: P3, [K1, P4, K1, P2, 1/1 LC, P2] 3x, K1, P4, K1, P3.
Row 15: Repeat row 13.
Row 16: P3, [K1, P4, K1, P1, 1/1 RPC, 1/1 LPC, P1] 3x, K1, P4, K1, P3.
Row 17: Repeat row 11.
Row 18: P3, [1/1 LPC, P2, 1/1 RPC x 2, P2, 1/1 LPC] 3x, 1/1 LPC, P2, 1/1 RPC, P3.
Row 19: K4, sl wyif, K2, sl wyif, K1, [sl wyif, K4, sl wyif, K1, sl wyif, K2, sl wyif, K1] 3x, K3.
Row 20: P3, [P1, (1/1 LPC, 1/1 RPC, P1, K1, P4, K1] 3x, P1, 1/1 LPC, 1/1 RPC, P4.
Row 21: Knit.
Row 22: Purl
Row 23: Knit
Row 24: Knit

Read the charts RS rows (even numbers) from right to left, and WS rows (odd numbers) from left to right.

DIRECTIONS

CO 48 sts. Work Rows 1-4 of chart once. Work Rows 7-20 of chart once. Work Rows 5-20 once. Work Rows 5-24 once. Do not bind off or turn work.

Pick Up Sts For I-cord BO

(Note: When skipping rows, do not include the live stitches or the cast on.)

With RS facing, rotate work 90 degrees to the right, PU and K48 from alongside the left edge of the dishcloth. [(1 st from each of the next 8 rows, skip a row) x 6], rotate work another 90 degrees to the right, PU and K48 from cast on edge, rotate work another 90 degrees to the right, PU and K48 from alongside the right edge of the dishcloth [(skip a row, PU and K1 from each of the next 8 rows) x 6]. 144 sts picked up plus 48 sts already on needle - 192 sts.

I-cord BO

With RS facing and using a DPN, knit in front loop of first st picked up, place on end of LH needle, knit in front loop of stitch just made, place on end of LH needle. 2sts inc.

(K1, K2tog TBL, place these 2 sts back onto LH needle) rep all around entire dishcloth until all sts have been worked. 2sts left on needle. Continue on to Loop instructions.

Loop

Using a second DPN, (slide 2 sts to right end of DPN, K2) rep until I-cord measures 3" long. Break yarn and sew down to beginning of I-cord.

Finishing

Weave in ends, wash and block to finished measurements.

Ceramic Chart

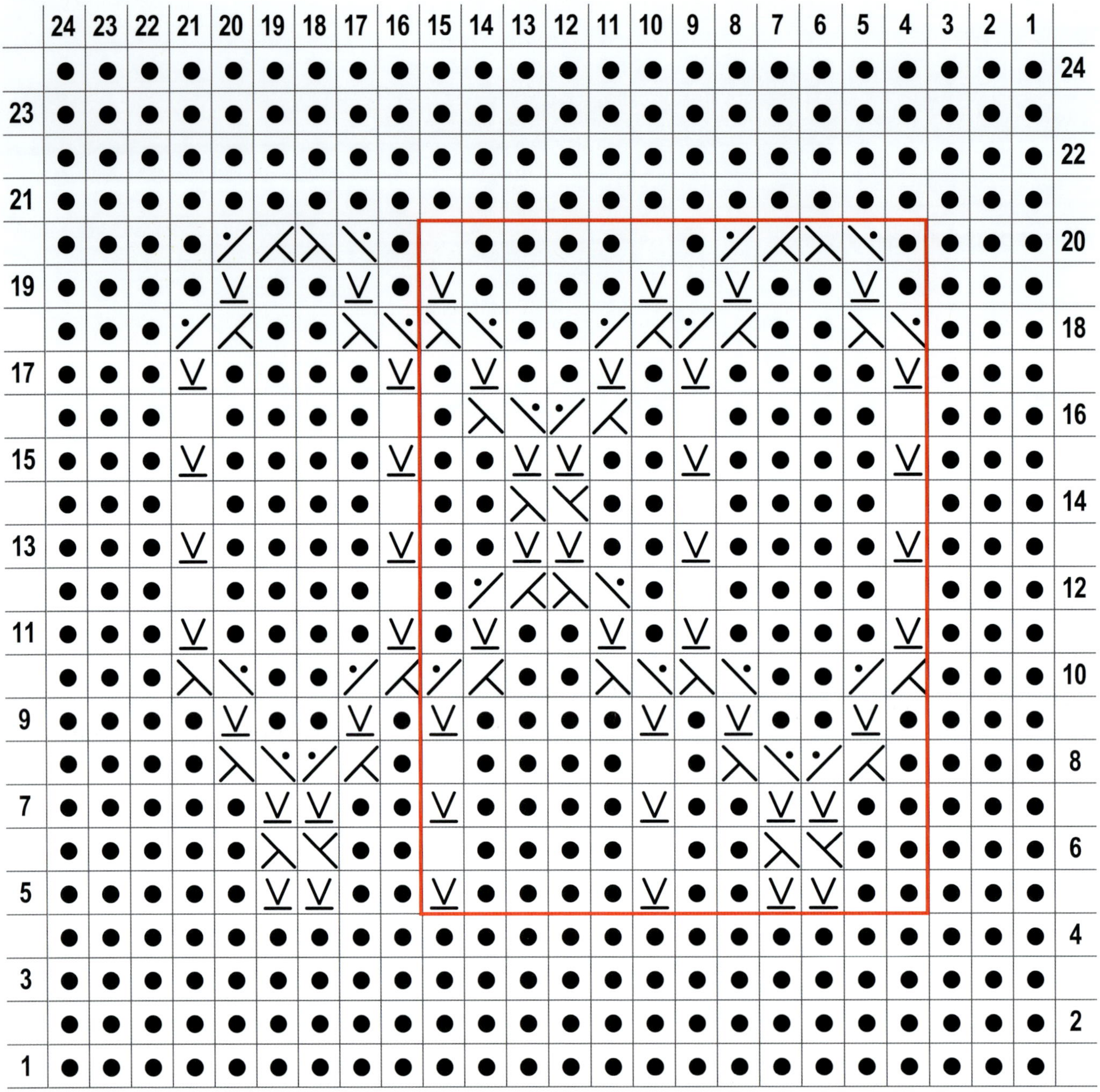

Legend

purl
RS: purl stitch
WS: knit stitch

slip wylf
WS: Slip stitch as if to purl, with yarn in front

1/1 LC
Knit into back of second stitch on LH knit into front loop of first stitch on LH needle, drop both sts off of LH needle

knit
RS: knit stitch
WS: purl stitch

1/1 LPC
WYIF, purl into back loop of second stitch on LH needle, bring yarn to front of work, knit in front loop of the first stitch on LH needle, drop both sts off of LH needle.

1/1 RPC
Skip first stitch on LH needle WYIB, knit through front loop of second stitch on LH needle, pull the stitch through to the front of work, bring yarn to the front of work, purl front loop of first stitch, drop both sts off of LH needle.

Pattern Repeat

SIMPLE EYELET WASHCLOTH

by Kendra Nitta

Knit up a pretty eyelet washcloth for a favorite teacher or beloved friend. A great way for newer knitters to take the first step on the road to lace! The yarn is held doubled throughout.

FINISHED MEASUREMENTS

Approximately 8.5" square, blocked

YARN

Knit Picks Lindy Chain (70% Linen, 30% Pima Cotton; 180 yards/50g): Blush 26464, 1 ball

NEEDLES

US 5 (3.75mm) straight or circular needles, or size to obtain gauge

NOTIONS

Yarn Needle

GAUGE

21 sts and 48 rows = 4" in Garter st, unblocked. Gauge for this project is approximate

Notes:

Garter St (worked flat over any number of sts)

All Rows: K.

DIRECTIONS

CO 45 sts with yarn held double.

Work in Garter st for 10 rows.

Row 1 (RS): K4, (YO, K2tog, K2) until last st, K1.

Row 2 (WS): K5, P35, K5.

Row 3: K5, (SSK, YO, K2) until last 4 sts, K4.

Row 4: K5, P35, K5.

Repeat Rows 1-4 until piece measures approximately 7.5" from CO edge, ending with Row 1 or 3.

Work in Garter st for 10 rows.

BO all sts.

Finishing

Weave in ends, wash and block to finished dimensions.

ZODIAC

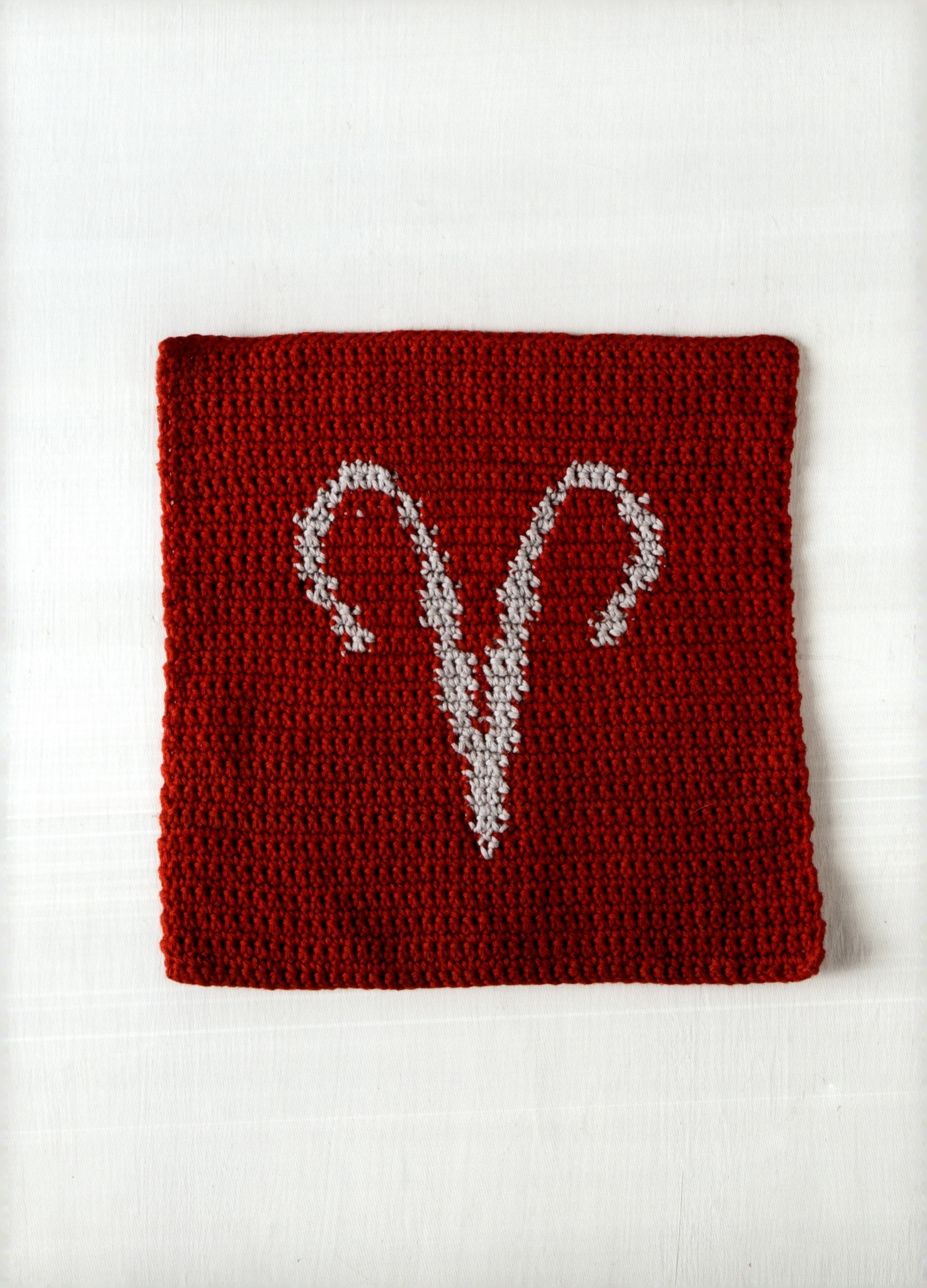

TAURUS

by Beth Major

Using crochet colorwork or tapestry crochet, each dishcloth in this series features a specific Zodiac design pattern in a fully charted format. The color of each dishcloth was chosen to reflect the specific color associated with each Zodiac sign. For the sign Taurus, the color Canary was chosen to represent the bright earthy yellow of Yellow Topaz.

FINISHED MEASUREMENTS

9.5" square, approximately

YARN

Knit Picks CotLin (70% Tanguis Cotton, 30% Linen; 123 yards/50g): MC Canary 24837, CC Wallaby 25775, 1 ball each

HOOK

G/6, 4.00 mm

NOTIONS

Yarn Needle
Stitch Markers

GAUGE

18 sts and 20 rows = 4" in SC, blocked

Notes:
The colorwork is done using the carrying method for the zodiac sign portion of the work only. At the end of the sign portion of each row, the contrasting color is wrapped to the front of the work so that it can be easily picked up in the next row.
For help using the carrying method in colorwork crochet, please refer to the following tutorial:
http://tutorials.knitpicks.com/colorwork-crochet-carrying-method/

DIRECTIONS

Row 1 (RS): With MC, CH 47, SC in 2nd CH from hook and in each CH across - 46 SC.
Row 2 (WS): Start working Taurus chart row 2: ch1, turn, SC in 2nd stitch from hook, SC crochet to end.
Cont working from Taurus chart in SC. Begin colorwork crochet on row 10 and cont through row 42.

Finishing

Fasten off. Weave in ends.

Taurus Chart

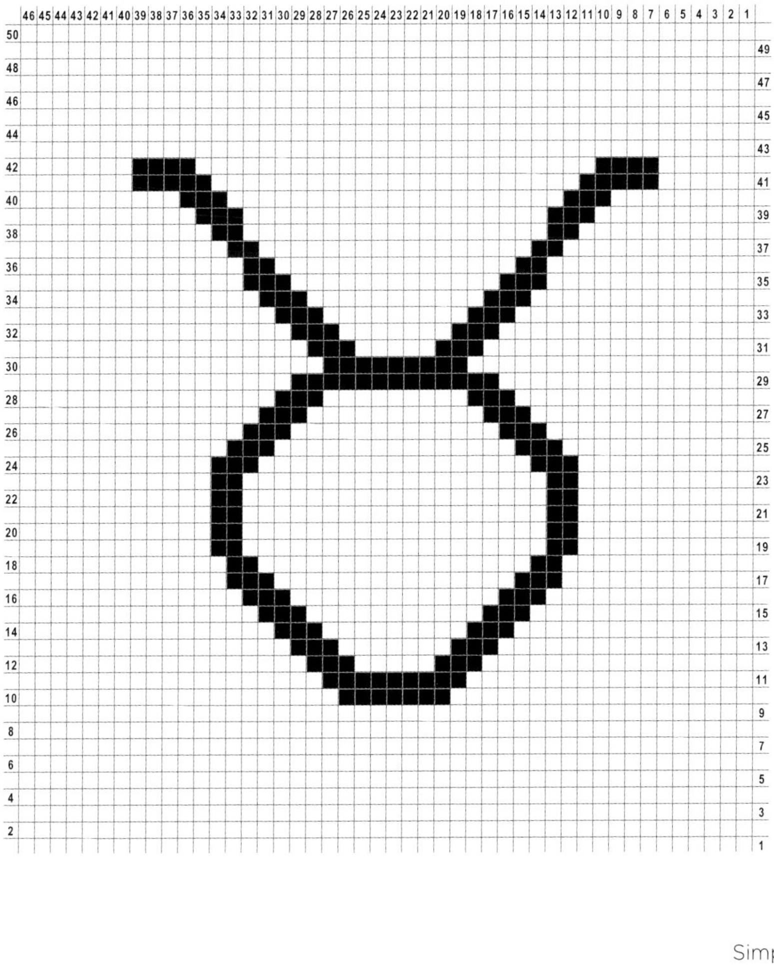

Legend

☐ MC

■ CC

GEMINI

by Beth Major

Using crochet colorwork or tapestry crochet, each dishcloth in this series features a specific Zodiac design pattern in a fully charted format. The color of each cloth was chosen to reflect the specific color associated with each Zodiac sign. For the sign Gemini, the color Crème Brûlée was chosen to represent the soft earthy yellow of Citrine.

FINISHED MEASUREMENTS
9.5" square, approximately

YARN
Knit Picks CotLin (70% Tanguis Cotton, 30% Linen; 123 yards/50g): MC Crème Brûlée 24137, CC Wallaby 25775, 1 ball each

HOOK
G/6, 4.00 mm

NOTIONS
Yarn Needle
Stitch Markers

GAUGE
18 sts and 20 rows = 4" in SC, blocked

Notes:
The colorwork is done using the carrying method for the zodiac sign portion of the work only. At the end of the sign portion of each row, the contrasting color is wrapped to the front of the work so that it can be easily picked up in the next row.
For help using the carrying method in colorwork crochet, please refer to the following tutorial:
http://tutorials.knitpicks.com/colorwork-crochet-carrying-method/

DIRECTIONS
Row 1 (RS): With MC, CH 47, SC in 2nd CH from hook and in each CH across - 46 SC.
Row 2 (WS): Start working Gemini chart row 2: ch1, turn, SC in 2nd stitch from hook, SC crochet to end.
Cont working from Gemini chart in SC. Begin colorwork crochet on row 9 and cont through row 42.

Finishing
Fasten off. Weave in ends.

Gemini Chart

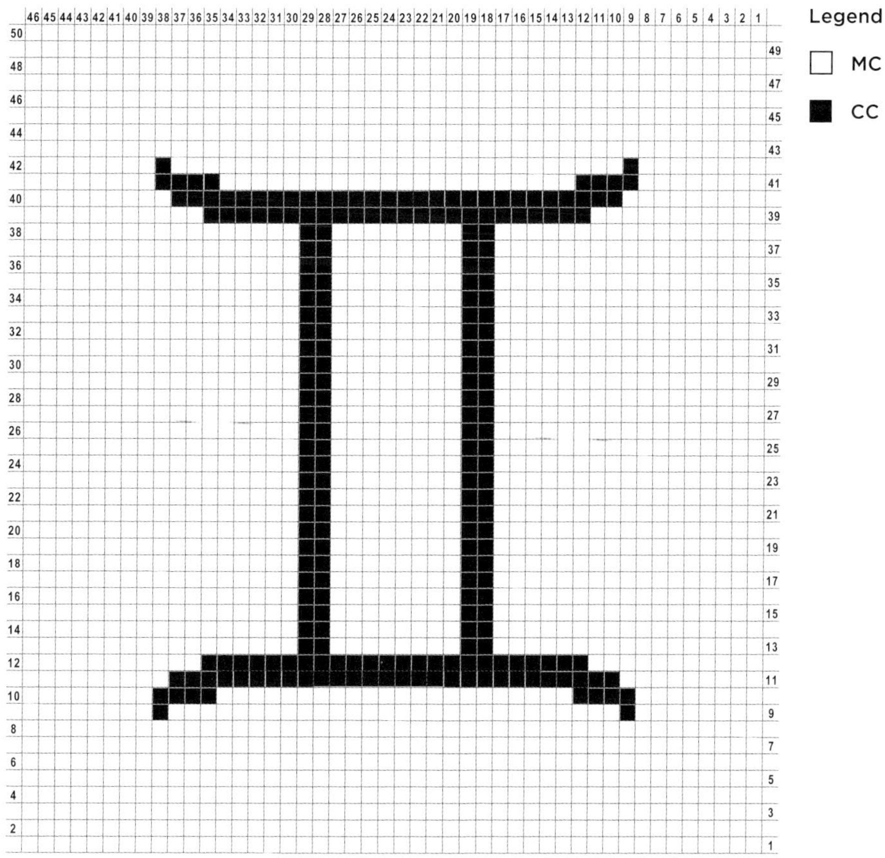

CANCER

by Beth Major

Using crochet colorwork or tapestry crochet, each dishcloth in this series features a specific Zodiac design pattern in a fully charted format. The color of each cloth was chosen to reflect the specific color associated with each Zodiac sign. For the sign Cancer, the color Whisper was chosen to represent the soft and delicate purple of Alexandrite.

FINISHED MEASUREMENTS
9.5" square, approximately

YARN
Knit Picks CotLin (70% Tanguis Cotton, 30% Linen; 123 yards/50g): MC Whisper 25328, CC Wallaby 25775, 1 ball each

HOOK
G/6, 4.00 mm

NOTIONS
Yarn Needle
Stitch Markers

GAUGE
18 sts and 20 rows = 4" in SC, blocked

Notes:
The colorwork is done using the carrying method for the zodiac sign portion of the work only. At the end of the sign portion of each row, the contrasting color is wrapped to the front of the work so that it can be easily picked up in the next row.
For help using the carrying method in colorwork crochet, please refer to the following tutorial:
http://tutorials.knitpicks.com/colorwork-crochet-carrying-method/

DIRECTIONS
Row 1 (RS): With MC, CH 47, SC in 2nd CH from hook and in each CH across - 46 SC.
Row 2 (WS): Start working Cancer chart row 2: ch1, turn, SC in 2nd stitch from hook, SC crochet to end.
Cont working from Cancer chart in SC. Begin colorwork crochet on row 11 and cont through row 40.

Finishing
Fasten off. Weave in ends.

Cancer Chart

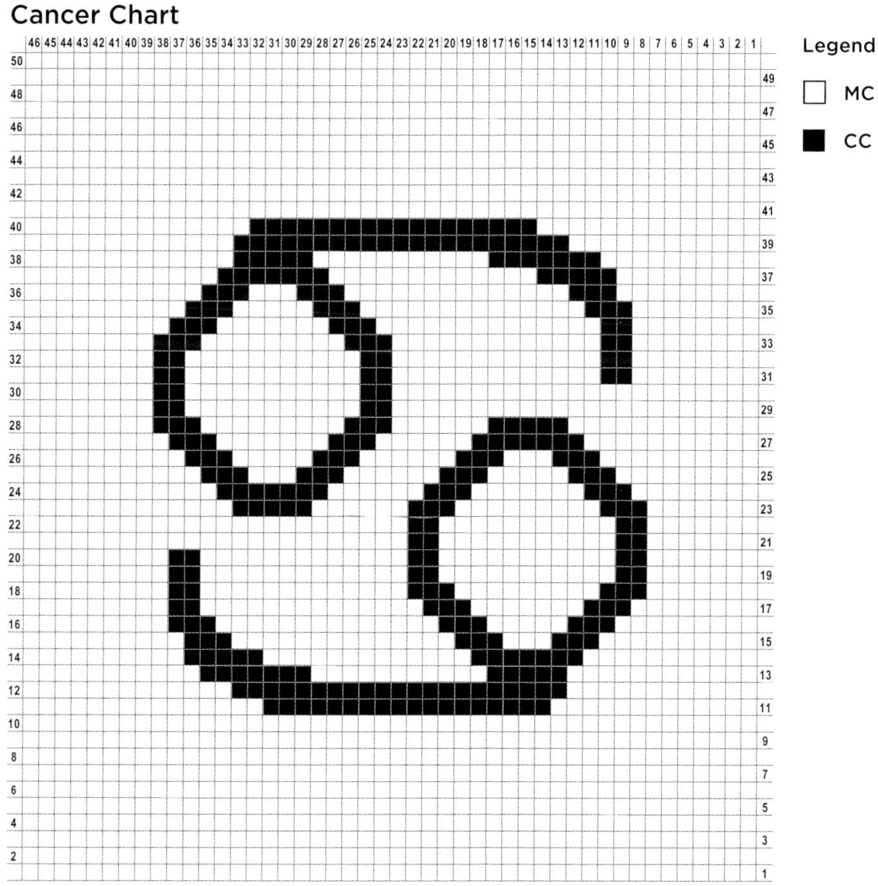

LIBRA

by Beth Major

Using crochet colorwork or tapestry crochet, each dishcloth in this series features a specific Zodiac design pattern in a fully charted format. The color of each cloth was chosen to reflect the specific color associated with each Zodiac sign. sign. For the sign Libra, the color Lichen was chosen to represent the soft earthy green of Peridot.

FINISHED MEASUREMENTS

9.5" square, approximately

YARN

Knit Picks CotLin (70% Tanguis Cotton, 30% Linen; 123 yards/50g): MC: Lichen 26674, C1: Wallaby 25775, 1 ball each

HOOK

G/6, 4.00 mm

NOTIONS

Yarn Needle
Stitch Markers

GAUGE

18 sts and 20 rows = 4" in SC, blocked

Notes:
The colorwork is done using the carrying method for the zodiac sign portion of the work only. At the end of the sign portion of each row, the contrasting color is wrapped to the front of the work so that it can be easily picked up in the next row.
For help using the carrying method in colorwork crochet, please refer to the following tutorial:
http://tutorials.knitpicks.com/colorwork-crochet-carrying-method/

DIRECTIONS

Row 1 (RS): With MC, CH 47, SC in 2nd CH from hook and in each CH across - 46 SC.
Row 2 (WS): Start working Libra chart row 2: ch1, turn, SC in 2nd stitch from hook, SC crochet to end.
Cont working from Libra chart in SC. Begin colorwork crochet on row 12 and cont through row 40.

Finishing

Fasten off. Weave in ends.

Libra Chart

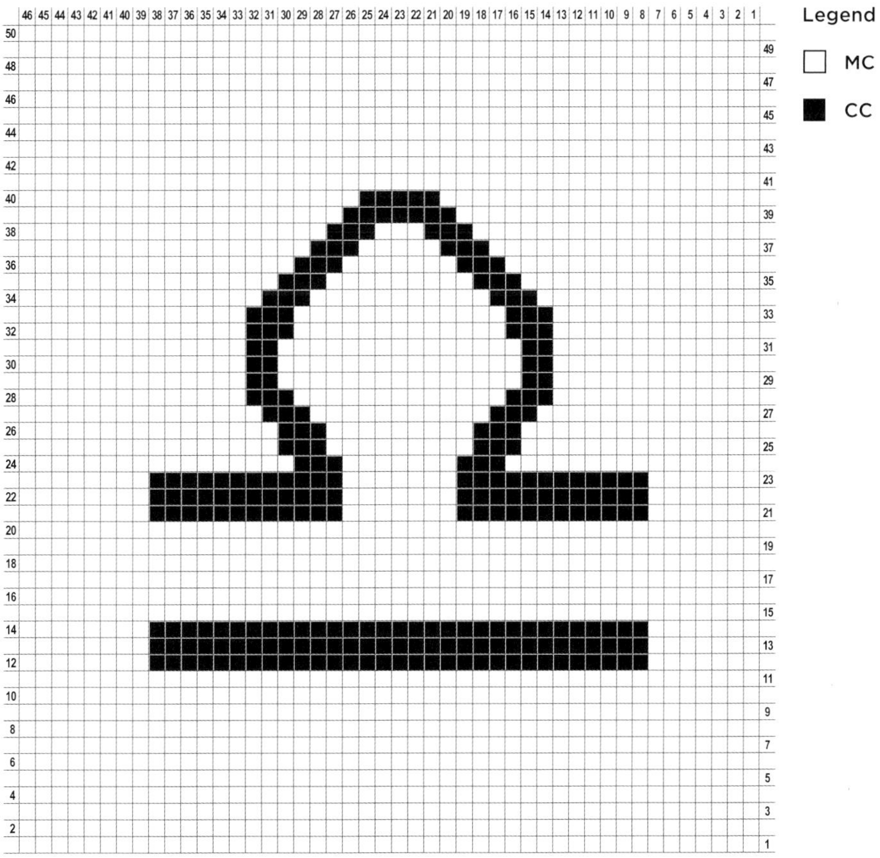

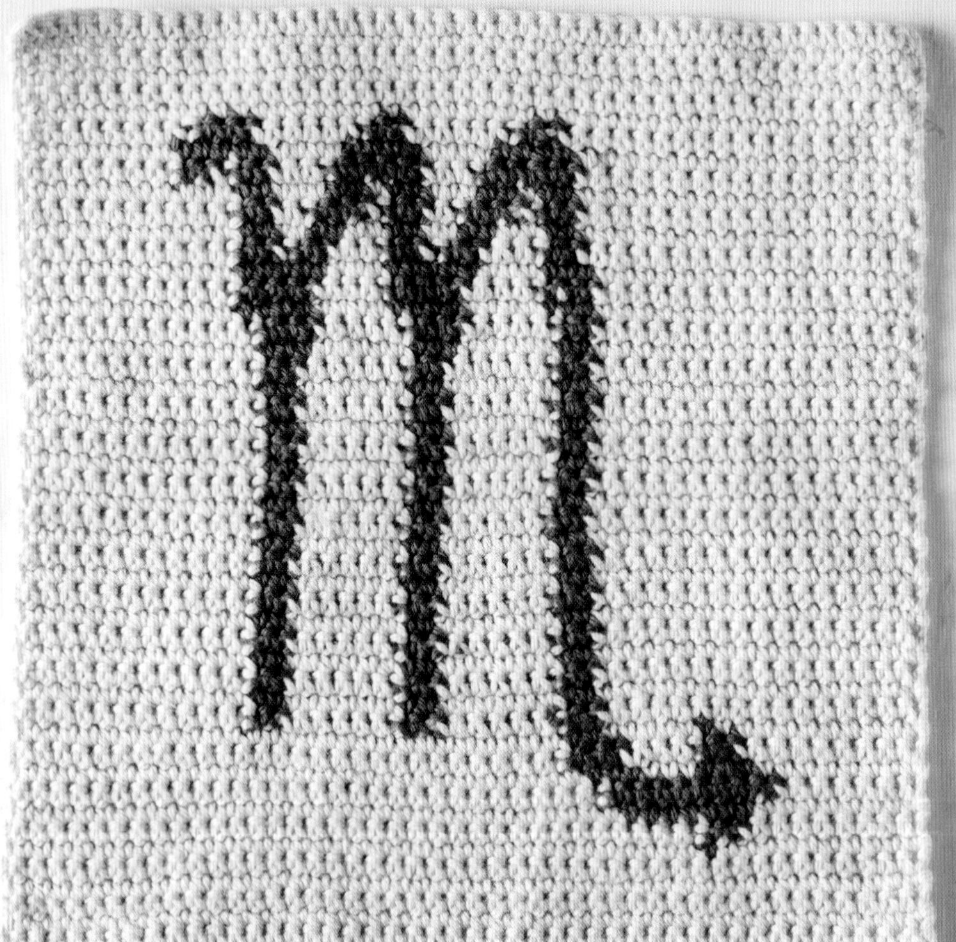

SCORPIO

by Beth Major

Using crochet colorwork or tapestry crochet, each dishcloth in this series features a specific Zodiac design pattern in a fully charted format. The color of each cloth was chosen to reflect the specific color associated with each Zodiac sign. sign. For the sign Scorpio, the color Clarity was chosen to represent the soft delicate blue of Aquamarine.

FINISHED MEASUREMENTS

9.5" square, approximately

YARN

Knit Picks CotLin (70% Tanguis Cotton, 30% Linen; 123 yards/50g): MC: Clarity 26997, C1: Wallaby 25775, 1 ball each

HOOK

G/6, 4.00 mm

NOTIONS

Yarn Needle
Stitch Markers

GAUGE

18 sts and 20 rows = 4" in SC, blocked

Notes:

The colorwork is done using the carrying method for the zodiac sign portion of the work only. At the end of the sign portion of each row, the contrasting color is wrapped to the front of the work so that it can be easily picked up in the next row.

For help using the carrying method in colorwork crochet, please refer to the following tutorial:
http://tutorials.knitpicks.com/colorwork-crochet-carrying-method/

DIRECTIONS

Row 1 (RS): With MC, CH 47, SC in 2nd CH from hook and in each CH across - 46 SC.

Row 2 (WS): Start working Scorpio chart row 2: ch1, turn, SC in 2nd stitch from hook, SC crochet to end.

Cont working from Scorpio chart in SC. Begin colorwork crochet on row 12 and cont through row 40.

Finishing

Fasten off. Weave in ends.

Scorpio Chart

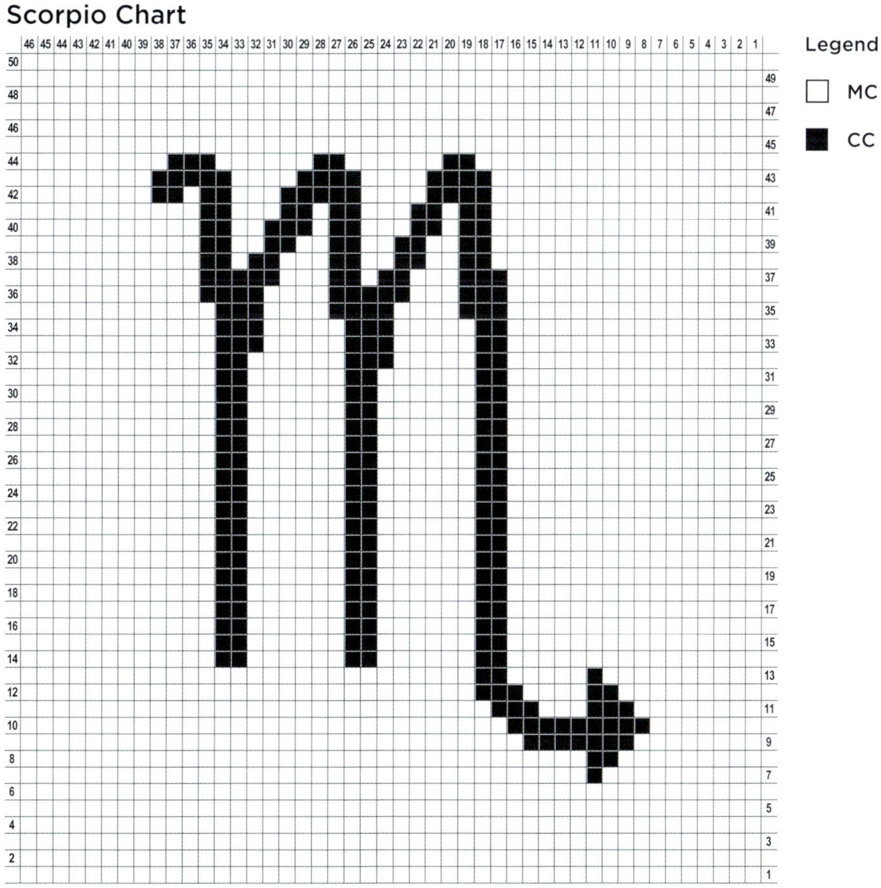

SAGITTARIUS

by Beth Major

Using crochet colorwork or tapestry crochet, each dishcloth in this series features a specific Zodiac design pattern in a fully charted format. The color of each cloth was chosen to reflect the specific color associated with each Zodiac sign. For the sign Sagittarius, the color Clementine was chosen to represent the bright orange of Orange Garnet.

FINISHED MEASUREMENTS
9.5" square, approximately

YARN
Knit Picks CotLin (70% Tanguis Cotton, 30% Linen; 123 yards/50g): MC: Clementine 24460, C1: Wallaby 25775, 1 ball each

HOOK
G/6, 4.00 mm

NOTIONS
Yarn Needle
Stitch Markers

GAUGE
18 sts and 20 rows = 4" in SC, blocked

Notes:
The colorwork is done using the carrying method for the zodiac sign portion of the work only. At the end of the sign portion of each row, the contrasting color is wrapped to the front of the work so that it can be easily picked up in the next row.
For help using the carrying method in colorwork crochet, please refer to the following tutorial:
http://tutorials.knitpicks.com/colorwork-crochet-carrying-method/

DIRECTIONS
Row 1 (RS): With MC, CH 47, SC in 2nd CH from hook and in each CH across - 46 SC.
Row 2 (WS): Start working Sagittarius chart row 2: ch1, turn, SC in 2nd stitch from hook, SC crochet to end.
Cont working from Sagittarius chart in SC. Begin colorwork crochet on row 12 and cont through row 39.

Finishing
Fasten off. Weave in ends.

Sagittarius Chart

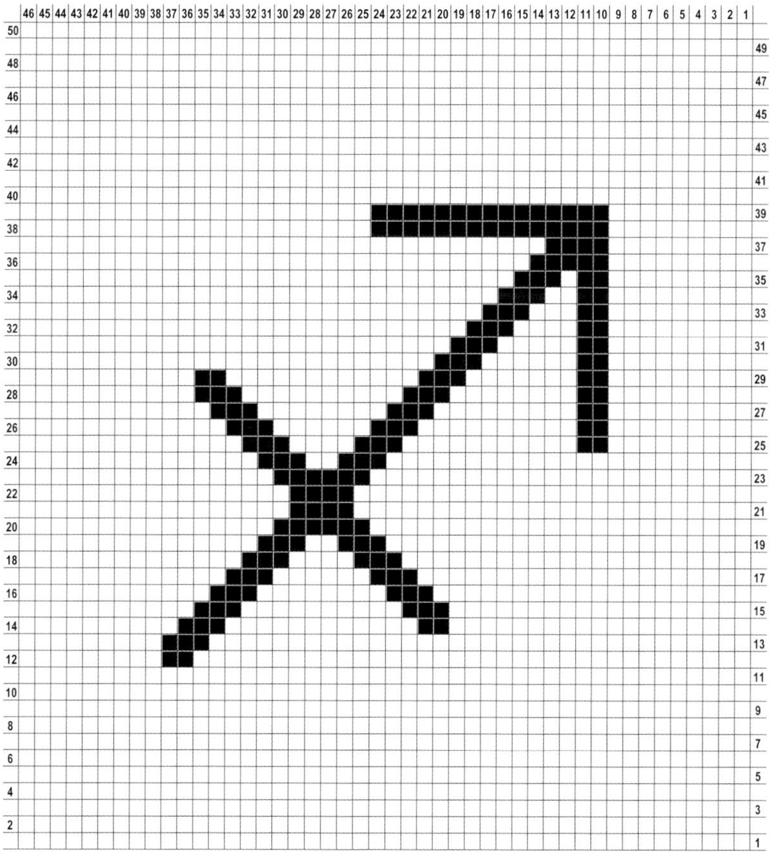

Legend

☐ MC

■ CC

CAPRICORN

by Beth Major

Using crochet colorwork or tapestry crochet, each dishcloth in this series features a specific Zodiac design pattern in a fully charted format. The color of each cloth was chosen to reflect the specific color associated with each Zodiac sign. For the sign Capricorn, the color Harbor was chosen to represent the deep earthy green-blue of Green Tourmaline.

FINISHED MEASUREMENTS

9.5" square, approximately

YARN

Knit Picks CotLin (70% Tanguis Cotton, 30% Linen; 123 yards/50g): MC: Harbor 24464, C1: Whisker 24834, 1 ball each

HOOK

G/6, 4.00 mm

NOTIONS

Yarn Needle
Stitch Markers

GAUGE

18 sts and 20 rows = 4" in SC, blocked

Notes:

The colorwork is done using the carrying method for the zodiac sign portion of the work only. At the end of the sign portion of each row, the contrasting color is wrapped to the front of the work so that it can be easily picked up in the next row.
For help using the carrying method in colorwork crochet, please refer to the following tutorial:
http://tutorials.knitpicks.com/colorwork-crochet-carrying-method/

DIRECTIONS

Row 1 (RS): With MC, CH 47, SC in 2nd CH from hook and in each CH across - 46 SC.
Row 2 (WS): Start working Capricorn chart row 2: ch1, turn, SC in 2nd stitch from hook, SC crochet to end.
Cont working from Capricorn chart in SC. Begin colorwork crochet on row 12 and cont through row 39.

Finishing

Fasten off. Weave in ends.

Capricorn Chart

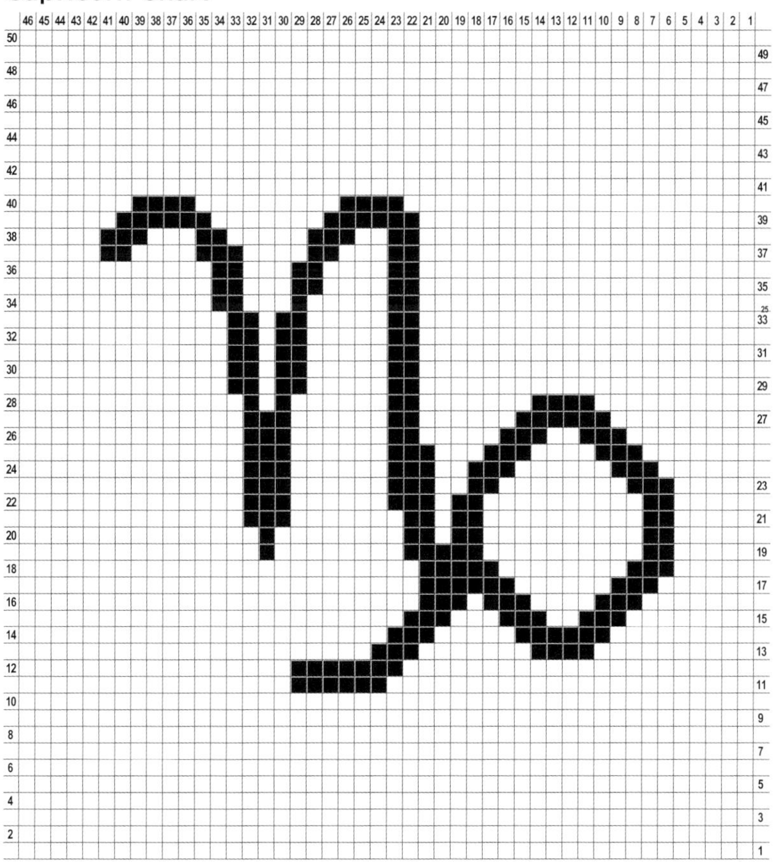

Legend

☐ MC

■ CC

AQUARIUS

by Beth Major

Using crochet colorwork or tapestry crochet, each cloth in this series features a specific Zodiac design pattern in a fully charted format. The color of each cloth was chosen to reflect the specific color associated with each Zodiac sign. For the sign Aquarius, the color Planetarium was chosen to represent the deep blue of the sapphire.

FINISHED MEASUREMENTS

9.5" square, approximately

YARN

Knit Picks CotLin (70% Tanguis Cotton, 30% Linen; 123 yards/50g): MC: Planetarium 24465, CC1: Whisker 24834, 1 ball each

HOOK

G/6, 4.00 mm

NOTIONS

Yarn Needle
Stitch Markers

GAUGE

18 sts and 20 rows = 4" in SC, blocked

Notes:

The colorwork is done using the carrying method for the zodiac sign portion of the work only. At the end of the sign portion of each row, the contrasting color is wrapped to the *front* of the work so that it can be easily picked up in the next row.
For help using the carrying method in colorwork crochet, , please refer to the following tutorial:
http://tutorials.knitpicks.com/colorwork-crochet-carrying-method/

DIRECTIONS

Row 1 (RS): With MC, CH 47, SC in 2nd CH from hook and in each CH across - 46 SC.
Row 2 (WS): Start working Aquarius Chart row 2: ch1, turn, SC in 2nd stitch from hook, SC crochet to end.
Cont working from Aquarius Chart in SC. Begin colorwork crochet. on row 11 and cont through row 40

Finishing

Fasten off. Weave in ends.

Aquarius Chart

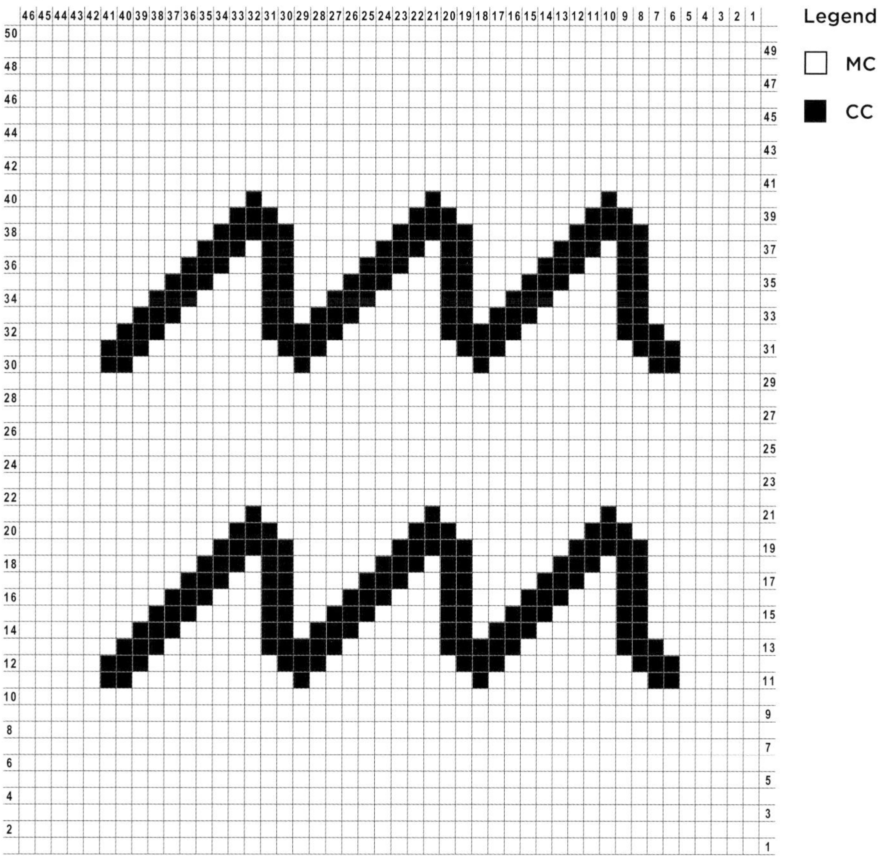

PISCES

by Beth Major

Using crochet colorwork or tapestry crochet, each cloth in this series features a specific Zodiac design pattern in a fully charted format. The color of each cloth was chosen to reflect the specific color associated with each Zodiac sign. For the sign Pisces, the color Lilac was chosen to represent the rich deep purple of amethyst.

FINISHED MEASUREMENTS

9.5" square, approximately

YARN

Knit Picks CotLin (70% Tanguis Cotton, 30% Linen; 123 yards/50g): MC: Lilac 24836, CC1: Whisker 24834, 1 ball each

HOOK

G/6, 4.00 mm

NOTIONS

Yarn Needle
Stitch Markers

GAUGE

18 sts and 20 rows = 4" in SC, blocked

Notes:

The colorwork is done using the carrying method for the zodiac sign portion of the work only. At the end of the sign portion of each row, the contrasting color is wrapped to the front of the work so that it can be easily picked up in the next row.

For help using the carrying method in colorwork crochet, please refer to the following tutorial: http://tutorials.knitpicks.com/colorwork-crochet-carrying-method/

DIRECTIONS

Row 1 (RS): With MC, CH 47, SC in 2nd CH from hook and in each CH across - 46 SC.

Row 2 (WS): Start working Picses chart row 2: ch1, turn, SC in 2nd stitch from hook, SC crochet to end.

Cont working from Pisces chart in SC. Begin colorwork crochet. on row 11 and cont through row 40.

Finishing

Fasten off. Weave in ends.

Pisces Chart

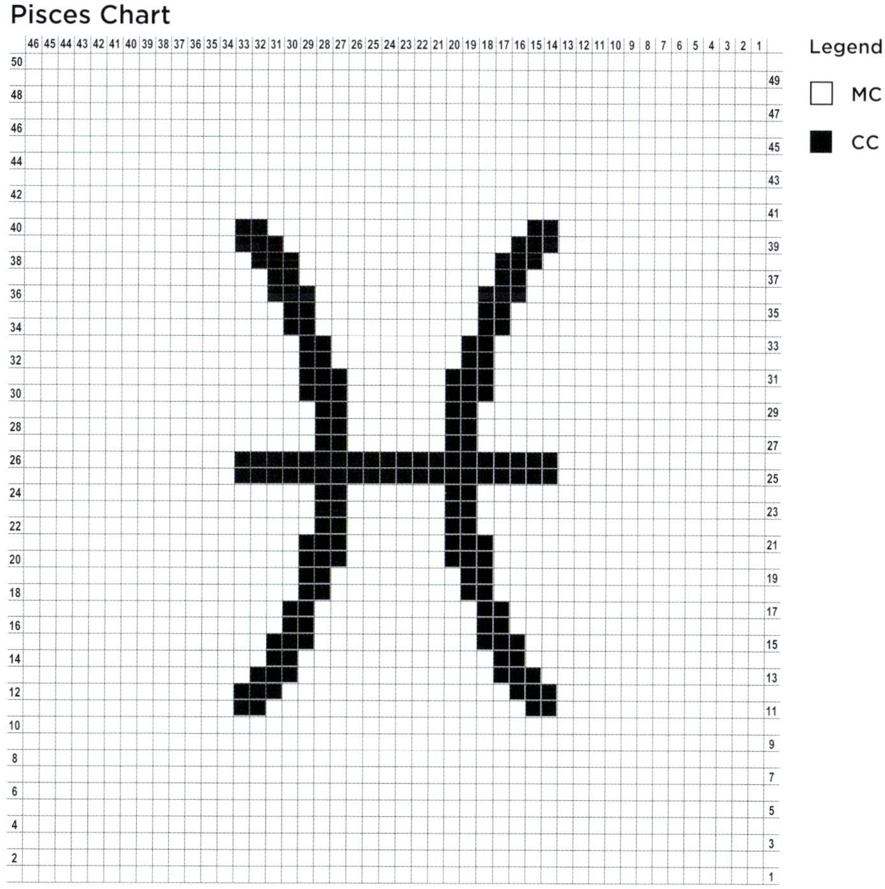

MEET THE DESIGNERS

Allyson Dykhuizen is a knitwear designer and knitting teacher from Michigan who lives in Chicago. Her patterns have been published in Interweave Knits, Knitscene, and knit.wear magazines, by Lion Brand Yarns, and included in the Knit Picks Independent Designer Program. She can be found on Ravelry at sweatshopoflove, self publishes and blogs on her website The Sweatshop of Love, and is editor of Holla Knits.
For pattern support, please contact allyson@thesweatshopoflove.com

Emily Ringelman lives in Baton Rouge, Louisiana, a place known more for alligators and gumbo than its knitting designers, but hey, a passion is a passion. Find her on Ravelry as EmilyRingelman.
For pattern support, please contact emily.ringelman@gmail.com

Faith Schmidt designs under the name DistractedKnits for a very good reason. With nine children in the house, there's always something going on! This has led her to design patterns that are interesting to knit, but are also easy to memorize and "read", in case of one of those all-too-frequent interruptions. Faith can be found online at http://DistractedKnits.weebly.com and on Ravelry, Pinterest, Instagram and Twitter as DistractedKnits.
For pattern support, please contact DistractedKnits@hotmail.com

Kalurah's love of the Fiber Arts budded from an early life surrounded by art. But knitting and crocheting has just recently become this Northwest Native's newest love. She learned from a friend in late 2008 and now designs her own knit and crochet creations. This happy wife and mom of 3 dreams of some day living on an Alpaca Farm and starting up a fiber studio with built in coffee bistro.
For pattern support, please contact kalurah@whiletheyplay.com

Kendra Nitta's handknit designs have been featured in numerous books and magazines, and are available through Knit Picks and on Ravelry. She also sews and designs quilts. Follow along at www.missknitta.com and @missknitta.
For pattern support, please contact missknitta@gmail.com

Allison Griffith is a lifelong knitter with years of experience designing patterns and teaching fiber arts. She is the creator and author of the blog On the Needles (www.ontheneedles.com) where she offers patterns, tutorials, and inspiration to hundreds of readers. When not knitting, Allison divides her time between working in her garden, watching too many Law & Order reruns, and playing with her dog.
For pattern support, please contact knittingontheneedles@gmail.com.

A former Assyriologist and state bureaucrat, **Ann Weaver** currently works as a bread baker. Her designs, inspired by her friends, family, and her own proto-punk aesthetic, can be found in print and internet publications like Interweave Knits and knitty.com. Her favorite things include dark beers, napping, cycling, and reading a wide variety of literature.
For pattern support, please contact weaverknits77@gmail.com.

Born and raised on eastern Long Island, NY, **Erica Jackofsky** grew up surrounded by the arts— performing (playing fiddle, flatfoot dancing, and singing) and traveling around the country with her family band, The Homegrown String Band. During her travels, Erica discovered knitting and crocheting and it wasn't long before the kid who fiddles to a different drummer was accumulating a yarn stash and designing her own projects. In early 2009 Erica established Fiddle Knits Designs and began to focus her energies on designing and creating original patterns inspired by music.
For pattern support, please contact Erica@FiddleKnits.com.

Joyce Fassbender is a biology lecturer in New York City. She recently got a puppy that she's training to be a good knitting dog, but not to knit because, sadly, it can't hold the needles. When not playing with the puppy, she's obsessing over shawls and lace.

For pattern support, please contact joycef2@gmail.com

Born in Sault Ste. Marie Ontario, **Beth Major** learned to crochet and knit at a young age from her Grandmother and while the needles confounded her, she really got hooked on crochet. Influenced by her upbringing in Northern Ontario, her designs tend to trend toward items for winter wear and home coziness. With a yarn stash that seems to breed in various closets and corners of her house, she often has at least 4 to 5 projects on the go at any one time and, when an idea sparks inspiration, will happily begin a new crochet project (or projects).

For pattern support, please contact crochetgypsy@gmail.com

Crochet Abbreviations

beg	beginning
BLP	single or double crochet in back loop only
BPDC	back post double crochet
ch(s)	chain(s)
ch-sp	chain space
DC	double crochet
FSC	foundation single crochet
FPDC	front post double crochet
HDC	half double crochet
lp(s)	loop(s)
PM	place marker
rem	remaining
rep	repeat
RM	remove marker
rnd(s)	round(s)
SC	single crochet
SC2tog	single crochet two together
shell	a group of stitches all worked in the same stitch
SL	slip
sl st	slip stitch
st(s)	stitch(es)
tr	treble crochet
TCH	top of turning chain made at the start of the previous row
YO	yarn over
••	repeat directions given from 'to'

Knit Abbreviations

BO	bind off
cn	cable needle
CC	contrast color
CDD	centered double dec
CO	cast on
cont	continue
dec	decrease(es)
DPN(s)	double pointed needle(s)
EOR	every other row
inc	increase
K	knit
K2tog	knit two sts together
KFB	knit into the front and back of stitch
K-wise	knitwise
LH	left hand
M	marker
M1	make one stitch
M1L	make one left-leaning stitch
M1R	make one right-lean-ing stitch
MC	main color
P	purl
P2tog	purl 2 sts together
PM	place marker
PFB	purl into the front and back of stitch
PSSO	pass slipped stitch over
PU	pick up
P-wise	purlwise
rep	repeat
Rev St st	reverse stockinette stitch
RH	right hand
rnd(s)	round(s)
RS	right side
Sk	skip
Sk2p	sl 1, k2tog, pass slipped stitch over k2tog: 2 sts dec
SKP	sl, k, psso: 1 st dec
SL	slip
SM	slip marker
SSK	sl, sl, k these 2 sts tog
SSP	sl, sl, p these 2 sts tog tbl
SSSK	sl, sl, sl, k these 3 sts tog
St st	stockinette stitch
sts	stitch(es)
TBL	through back loop
TFL	through front loop
tog	together
W&T	wrap & turn (see specific instructions in pattern)
WE	work even
WS	wrong side
WYIB	with yarn in back
WYIF	with yarn in front
YO	yarn over

Knit Picks yarn is both luxe and affordable—a seeming contradiction trounced! But it's not just about the pretty colors; we also care deeply about fiber quality and fair labor practices, leaving you with a gorgeously reliable product you'll turn to time and time again.

THIS COLLECTION FEATURES

DISHIE
Worsted Weight
100% Cotton

COTLIN
DK Weight
70% Tanguis Cotton, 30% Linen

SHINE
Worsted & Sport Weight
60% Pima Cotton, 40% Modal

COMFY
Worsted, Sport & Fingering Weight
75% Pima Cotton, 25% Acrylic

LINDY CHAIN
Fingering Weight
70% Linen, 30% Pima Cotton

View these beautiful yarns and more at www.Knit Picks.com